Thinking
Through
Primary Teaching

by

Steve Higgins

with

Viv Baumfield

and

David Leat
Series Editor
University of Newcastle

Chris Kington Publishing

CAMBRIDGE

© Steve Higgins
2001
Reprinted with minor alterations 2003

ISBN 1 899857 39 7

First published 2001 by
Chris Kington Publishing
27 Rathmore Road
Cambridge CB1 7AB

British Library cataloguing in publication data.

A catalogue record for this book is available from the British Library.

Printed in the United Kingdom by:
Halstan Ltd, Buckinghamshire.

Designed by:
Character Design, Hereford.

Thinking
Through
Primary Teaching

by
Steve Higgins
with
Viv Baumfield
and
David Leat,
Series Editor
University of Newcastle

With the support of:

Frank Hardman University of Newcastle
Maria Mroz University of Newcastle
Jen Miller University of Newcastle
Nick Packard North Tyneside LEA
Mel Rockett Northumberland LEA
Heather Shaw Sunderland LEA
Ian Thompson University of Newcastle

Teachers from Broomley, Mickley, Ovingham and Wylam First Schools, Northumberland:
**Moira Carr, Ursula Donnelly, Grahame Downey, Fay Hartland, Anne Hawes, Val High,
Linda Holden, Hanneke Jones, Lucy Lillico, Chris McGuire, Dorothy McSorley, Kirsty Roberts,
Julie Shields, Angela Steele, Lynn Telford, Gillian Woodworth, Barbara Wright**

Jenny Sloyan Archbishop Runcie First School, Newcastle

Irene Tomkinson Humshaugh Church of England First School

Teachers from North Tyneside: **Kerry Gamble, Karen Morgan, Joan Slade, Judith Williams**

Special thanks go to

Emma Packard of Stephenson Memorial First School in North Tyneside
for allowing us to use her artwork for some of the Resource Sheets.

CONTENTS

SECTION 2 APPROACHES

SECTION 3 EFFECTIVE TEACHING AND TEACHING THINKING

1
Thinking Through Primary Teaching

'Is the purpose of education to be improving economic conditions,
supplying a better grade of labour for the present scheme, or
aiding the country in a competitive struggle for world commerce?
Is its primary objective merely to prepare more skilled workers for
the present system or rather to develop human beings who are
equipped to think for themselves and reconstruct that scheme as
well as to realise their own best potentialities?'

John Dewey *Essays (1916-17)*

Introduction

'Developing better thinking and reasoning skills may have as much to do with creating dispositions for good thinking as it has to do with acquiring specific skills and strategies. For this reason classrooms need to have open-minded attitudes about the nature of knowledge and thinking and to create an educational atmosphere where talking about thinking - questioning, predicting, contradicting, doubting - is not only tolerated but actively pursued.

Increasingly it is recognised that developing thinking skills has implications not only for pupils' thinking but for teacher development and teacher thinking as well as for the ethos of schools as learning communities.'

McGuinness (1999)

This book is about effective primary teaching. It is about developing children's thinking and understanding of their own learning. It is also about supporting teachers in understanding their pupils' thinking and learning. The book arises from the work of the Thinking Skills Research Centre at Newcastle University and the team of researchers engaged in support, development and research into teaching thinking. It has been undertaken in partnership with teachers in the North East of England. We plan to achieve these aims for the book through providing ideas, structures and practical activities to focus attention on particular aspects of teaching and learning. We believe these aspects are essential for effective teaching: effective both in the short term to support the mantra of 'raising standards'; and effective in the longer term in helping pupils to become more effective learners.

Two key beliefs underpin this approach. The first is in the complexity of classrooms and in the complexity of the teaching and learning process. Whilst it is clearly essential to have teaching objectives and short-term subject outcomes for the hour or so of a lesson, it is even more essential that these hour long segments are connected by longer term aims that develop each pupil's skills, attitude and disposition to learning. The danger in an objective-led curriculum is that you don't see the wood for the trees and that the learners cannot connect the pieces of learning to each other and to their experience outside school. Like Mencken's adage: *'For every complex problem* (in this case classroom teaching) *there is a solution that is simple, neat* (three objectives with observable outcomes per hour) *and wrong.'* And, we believe, fundamentally wrong. It is dangerous and damaging to the complex professional skills of primary teachers.

The second belief is in the importance of language, discussion and social relationships in primary teaching. Effective teachers build effective learning relationships with pupils that develop over the course of (in most cases) a year of schooling. These teachers help pupils to develop connections within their learning and bridge this learning to their pupils' personal experience. The commitment, enthusiasm and belief of a teacher in the ability to succeed of each pupil communicates itself to pupils in subtle ways. The genuineness of interest a teacher shows in a pupil's response and of pupils' responses to each other communicates powerfully to encourage pupils' belief in themselves as learners. Learning needs to be brought out into the open, discussed, nurtured and celebrated so that pupils realise that their teacher may have taught them, but that they have done the learning!

Primary teaching should be exciting, challenging and stimulating for both pupils and teachers. The aim of this book is to support this goal. The Approaches and Strategies in this book are not without risk, however. Although they have been tried and tested in classrooms they do not come with guarantees of success. Indeed, the authors have on occasion tried them and experienced them falling flat! But, our usual experience is that pupils enjoy them and that teachers find the suggestions invigorating.

This book is therefore about professional development too. Making the Strategies and Approaches work effectively requires you to take risks to develop new classroom approaches and strategies and to learn more about children's learning.

Background

The book has arisen from the work of the Thinking Skills Research Centre at Newcastle University. We began by investigating published thinking skills programmes to identify what was powerful about them for teachers and learners. In this work we started to apply what we learned with the help of some enthusiastic (and patient) teachers. In particular the book draws on David Leat's work, whose ideas inspired teachers to infuse thinking skills strategies into the secondary geography curriculum and resulted in the publication of *Thinking Through*

Geography (1998). At the same time we have worked with groups of teachers in the North East of England and used the teaching of thinking as a focus for professional development The development and application of the Strategies and Approaches that we describe here owes much to these teachers, their enthusiasm and their dedication.

Levels of use

We have planned this book so that it can be used in different ways and at different Levels. Each Level makes progressively greater demands on teaching but the potential benefits to pupils and teachers are also greater.

Level 1: Using or applying the teaching resources

You can use the activities as they are described together with the photocopiable resources to create more interesting and challenging lessons. You might try an **Odd One Out** activity in mathematics using a numeracy target board *(see Resource 1)*. Or you might use the **Community of Enquiry** Approach with a story or literacy hour text to develop text level work with a focus on pupils' questioning skills. You could photocopy the **Living Graph** *Eureka!* and the accompanying statements to use with your class *(Resources 5 and 6)*.

Level 2: Adaptation and development

At the next Level you might choose to take the ideas and apply them in different contexts. The Strategy **Odd One Out**, for example, could be developed for other objectives in mathematics and science or could be transferred to other subjects such as history or art. At this Level our intention is that teachers take the Exemplars and use them to stimulate their own creativity. **Writing Frames** are helpful in supporting pupils to structure their writing of different kinds of texts and can easily and quickly be made by hand or using a computer. At this Level the feedback from pupils' engagement with the tasks starts to inform the teacher's assessment of their understanding and feeds forward into future tasks.

Level 3: Debriefing learning and metacognition

At the next Level you add **debriefing**. This means setting aside time in lessons, perhaps in **plenaries**, to discuss Strategies with pupils. This might be structured with:

- *what did you do?*
- *how did you do it?*
- *why was that effective/a good approach?*

Thinking about thinking, and talking about thinking is described as **metacognition**. It is through this process that learners start to gain insight into their own and other's thinking and learning. They may, for example, build up an understanding of specific important ideas in a particular subject. The **Odd One Out** science task could be used to help pupils identify and use appropriate scientific terminology for **classification**, for instance. Similarly, discussing mental calculation strategies in mathematics develops a metacognitive vocabulary so that pupils can identify a *type* of calculation. One example might be talking about *'doubles'* of single digit numbers. This can then be developed to identify *'near doubles'* to help children remember trickier calculations, such as $7 + 8$. It can also be discussed again in the context of two or three digit calculations, particularly for multiples of ten or a hundred (eg $40 + 40$ or $300 + 300$). Talking about a mental calculation strategy in this way provides a kind of shorthand that helps pupils apply, generalise and transfer particular techniques to other situations. This also works in other areas of the curriculum. **Writing Frames** can be used at two Levels. They can structure pupils' writing by increasing the *implicit* support given to different aspects of specific genres of writing. They can also be used *explicitly* to make this structuring part of the teaching and learning discussion so that pupils are made aware of how the **Writing Frame** has been used to help them structure their writing. This explicitness helps pupils to transfer their learning to other contexts. The teacher supports this process by encouraging the pupils to make connections with their experience or with other areas of learning, **bridging** from what has been learned to other knowledge and experience.

The teaching thinking Strategies in the book can therefore be used to develop a **vocabulary** *of* **learning** in and across particular subjects. And to develop a **vocabulary** *for* **learning** as pupils become increasingly familiar with talking about and understanding their own learning and the techniques and approaches that work for them.

Level 1 Application
of the activities.

Level 2 Adaptation
of the ideas and Strategies but with different content.

Level 3 Metacognition
or 'debriefing' the learning by talking about the Strategies and Approaches with pupils.

Level 4 Infusion
by adopting a whole school approach.

Developing a vocabulary **of** and **for** learning is **metacognition**.

Our experience suggests that this is hard to do, for all kinds of reasons. It is difficult to leave sufficient time for effective **bridging** and **debriefing** at the end of a session, particularly if the earlier stages of a lesson either are (or are not) going well. The children often realise that the **plenary** is a signal for the lesson to end and thoughts of playtime, lunch or home can be distracting. It may be more effective to stop the lesson to talk about these issues as they arise. It may be helpful to discuss some of them at the beginning of another session. This will then help to focus pupils' attention on how they are going to do it next time: that is, *now!*

Level 4: Total infusion

Infusion is where a whole school approach is required. A school might identify opportunities to integrate these Approaches and Strategies across the curriculum and progressively with different year groups. In addition there would need to be some commitment for professional development and INSET to develop classroom practice. **Integrating** or **infusing** teaching thinking approaches also needs changes in assessment policies and practices as well as in schemes of work.

Such an approach could include work on similarities and differences in Reception (4 - 5 year olds) and Year 1 (5 - 6 year olds) as well as **Community of Enquiry** with familiar stories and picture books. More emphasis on counting and less on sorting and ordering shapes and colours is recommended for young children in the *Framework for Mathematics* in England. Such an approach may well improve children's use of number. However, such activities are still essential to develop **classification** and **logical thinking**. Simple planning tools and **writing frames** can help pupils start to structure stories or other writing (for instance, by being able to talk about the beginning, middle and end, or write simple descriptions of characters).

In Year 2 (6 - 7 year olds) pupils would benefit from **Odd One Out** being developed more systematically so that they can identify corresponding similarities to the differences that they notice. They should also be able to discuss what sort of questions are good to discuss. Simple **Fortune Lines** and **Living Graphs** can be used, particularly if these have picture clues to support less fluent readers.

Each of these Approaches can be developed in Years 3 and 4 (7 - 9 year olds). It can be hard to assess children's understanding of scientific terminology or mathematical vocabulary: **Odd One Out** can be a good technique to provide formative or diagnostic information at the beginning of a unit of work, or to provide summative evidence of what has been learned. **Fortune Lines** and **Living Graphs** can be used with more complex information or in other areas of the curriculum. **Writing Frames** are invaluable with this age group to support continued development of skills. Nothing is more daunting than a blank page! Such support can help pupils to see themselves as improving, rather than failed, writers.

In Years 5 and 6 (9 - 11 year olds) all of the Strategies can be applied. More fluent readers with good collaborative skills can also manage **Mysteries**. In a **Community of Enquiry** they should also be able to distinguish between their reasoning and a particular argument and what the class might consider to be *reasonable*.

Challenges

A number of pressures militate against more systematic development and infusion of teaching thinking approaches. The space for professional development in England outside of National, OFSTED and LEA agendas in primary schools is sparse. We have therefore written this book with the expectation that most teachers will use it at Levels 1 and 2. The case studies in the book follow broadly these stages. The first examples of Strategies in *Section 1* of the book, such as **Odd One Out**, **Fortune Lines** or **Writing Frames**, are starting points which can be used in many classrooms as single lessons. These Strategies are also easy to adapt with different content for all age groups.

Community of Enquiry is an Approach which can be developed with a number of aims, but requires some commitment to developing the Approach over several weeks or a term. Some aspects of **metacognition** and **debriefing** are discussed in *Section 2*. **Meet the Zoombinis**, an Exemplar about ICT and logical thinking, attempts to integrate through **infusion** a number of strands for effective teaching, using **strategies** (or heurisitics), **debriefing** and explicit **bridging** into other areas of the curriculum.

Effective professional development

Section 3 makes a robust defence of the relevance of underpinning theories about learning and curriculum development to our work. The pendulum has swung dangerously far towards a technicist curriculum delivery model for teachers. This puts teaching at the mercy of political change, and the whims of accountability judgements. A teaching thinking curriculum allows a degree of resistance to these forces. This is because your understanding of *what* works and *why* enables you to keep a clear focus on what is effective for your teaching and your pupils' learning. Research on effective teaching and learning therefore informs the Strategies and Approaches in this book. As researchers we feel it is important that teachers test out the findings of our and others' research by trying out new approaches, or 'enacting' that research for themselves in their own classrooms.

Engagement in and with research is an important part of professional teaching. Being informed in this area helps you to defend what you do against both short-term fads and external political pressure to conform to a particular view of effectiveness. The literature we reviewed is extensive, complex, and, at times, contradictory. However, by keeping an eye on the big picture, the long term goals and intentions of education, it is possible to draw out practical implications to inform your teaching. Such research may also cause 'cognitive conflict' and force us to examine the beliefs and preconceptions about what we think effective teaching is. This conflict and reappraisal can lead to new insights and understanding.

Our review of the literature on effective teaching includes a substantial number of references and an academic bibliography. We acknowledge that this makes it heavier reading, but consider it vital to expose the research with which teaching thinking connects and intend that it will support those undertaking classroom-based research into effective teaching. The interest in teaching thinking as a basis for classroom research has grown enormously over the past few years and this section should support teachers in exploring some of the issues and ideas in greater depth.

We also think that it is the professional teacher's responsibility to make choices about *exactly what* to teach, *precisely when* it is appropriate to teach it, and *exactly how* to achieve teaching goals. This, of course, happens in a particular context. Pupils have an entitlement and schools have a responsibility to parents and to the society that funds them. But as professional educators we also have a responsibility to improve the effectiveness of what we do. Everyone in education is too busy; the burdens of paperwork are extreme. But at the same time it is essential for teachers to understand and to know how to help children to learn and to help them to become effective learners: it is this understanding which justifies the status of teaching as a profession. This is also the basis for our title: *Thinking Through Primary Teaching* – thinking it through as we teach and value pupils' thinking.

Strategies and Approaches: overview

Overview

This book is divided into three main Sections. *Section 1* and *Section 2* are the **Strategies** described in *Chapters 2 - 6* and the **Approaches** described in *Chapters 7 - 10*. This aim of this (rather arbitrary) distinction is to provide support for the Levels of use described in the *Introduction*. *Chapter 2* on *Introducing the Strategies* should get you started at Levels 1 and 2, *Chapter 7* on *Developing the Approaches* should help those who want to develop the ideas in more depth, and therefore support the move on to Levels 3 and 4. As far as possible each of the Sections and Exemplars is designed to stand alone so that the different chapters can be dipped into as a source of ideas or used in a different order from the way that they are presented. As a result of this some of the key ideas are repeated in different chapters.

Section 3 covers *Chapters 11 - 14*. Chapters on *Effective Teaching and Teaching Thinking* and on *Making it Work* cover issues to do with the research on teacher's effectiveness, classroom talk and professional development which underpin our thinking about the research and evidence base for our principles of teaching thinking. Further chapters and an *Appendix* offer information which we hope will be helpful: about metacognition; suggestions for developing resources with ICT; and information about teaching thinking on the World Wide Web.

The **Strategies** aim to get you started.

The Approaches support infusion of teaching thinking into the curriculum.

Introducing Strategies

Five **Strategies** for teaching thinking are described and exemplified though Exemplars in *Section 1*. The Strategies are:

Odd One Out

Fortune Lines

Living Graphs

Mysteries

Writing Frames

These Strategies have developed as part of the work of the Thinking Skills Research Centre at Newcastle University. They build on the work of other researchers and teachers involved in curriculum development. The Strategies are powerful as they represent techniques that can be applied across subjects and age groups. They are an excellent way to begin to 'teach thinking'.

Developing Approaches

Three chapters about teachers and schools starting to develop teaching thinking more widely follow in *Section 2*. These case studies describe:

Community of Enquiry

Developing mental calculation strategies through metacognition

Using ICT to support thinking and reasoning

These descriptions of **Approaches** offer examples of how teaching thinking can be integrated into effective teaching. This can be either across a school or group of schools, or by a teacher extending the Strategies across the curriculum. At this point teaching thinking starts to merge with professional development because the ideas developed through teaching thinking are at the heart of effective teaching and learning.

Principles of teaching thinking

Section 3 underlies the previous two Sections and details some principles of teaching thinking. Following on from the Newcastle research, we have analysed common features identified from studying the implementation of some of the published schemes and programmes for teaching thinking skills. We have developed these principles through the explicit teaching of thinking from our work with teachers across the North East of England.

Clear purpose

The purposes of tasks are made explicit as part of the teaching process and these aims are, at least in part, understood by pupils. This helps to provide pupils with specific targets that they can achieve and can reflect on. This means helping pupils to understand not just *what* they have to do, but *why* they are doing it. This can be enhanced by some negotiation with pupils about the particular focus of activities, such as identifying the questions for discussion in a **Community of Enquiry**.

Articulation

Pupils talk about their work and are encouraged to describe and articulate their thinking. This has several benefits. From the teacher's point of view, you get a chance to hear how pupils are thinking as they explain their reasoning. This is an opportunity to address any misconceptions or to develop their thinking. For the pupils, talking is usually seen as 'easy', but they get the chance to change their minds in the light of what others say.

Mediation

The teacher intervenes to discuss the learning that is taking place (and perhaps involves pupils in this through modelling and collaborative work). In this way the teacher 'mediates' the learning. This includes whole class explanation and discussion as well as direct teaching.

Connecting learning

The teacher and pupils make connections both within the tasks, between tasks and with their wider experience. This is sometimes described as **bridging** of learning by the teacher to encourage **transfer** of learning for pupils. Connecting learning starts to change the conceptions of teaching as bounded by lessons and summative assessments.

Evaluation

Pupils evaluate their own performance. Only once the purpose of learning is meaningfully understood, can pupils start to evaluate how successful they have been and then identify why they were successful or unsuccessful.

Metacognition

The teacher and pupils discuss and evaluate the learning that has taken place. This supports pupils in seeing themselves as successful learners and able to learn rather than just accepting that they are either good at it or not. It also helps to develop an understanding of learning strategies, styles or approaches that may help them in future learning.

Suggestions for further reading

Interest in teaching thinking and thinking skills has been growing steadily. In the UK, Carol McGuinness' (1999) report for the Department for Education and Employment has proved to be a significant step in making thinking skills more explicit in the curriculum. It is entitled *From Thinking Skills to Thinking Classrooms: a review and evaluation of approaches for developing pupils' thinking* (London: DFEE Research Report RR115 (ISBN 1 84185 013 6)). It is (or was) available on the web at: http://www.dfee.gov.uk/research/report115.html.

This is an international development, however, and a more general background can be found in the following books:

Baron J.B. & Sternberg R.J.

(eds) (1987) *Teaching Thinking Skills, Theory and Practice* New York: Freeman

Coles M.J. & Robinson

(1989) *Teaching Thinking* Bristol: Bristol Press

Collins C. & Mangieri J.N.

(1992) *Teaching Thinking: An Agenda for the Twenty-First Century* Hillsdale, NJ: Lawrence Erlbaum

Resnick L.B. & Klopfer L.E.

(eds) (1989) *Toward the Thinking Curriculum: Current Cognitive Research* Alexandria, VA: Association for Supervision and Curriculum Development

Other research and development in education also indicated that the explicit teaching of thinking and reasoning is an effective and important part of education. Our work is particularly influenced by research on classroom language and discourse as well as work on formative assessment and metacognition. The following books and articles help to set teaching thinking in this broader educational context:

Barnes D. & Todd F.

(1995) *Communication and Learning Revisited: Making Meaning Through Talk* Portsmouth, NH: Heinemann

Black P. & Wiliam D.

(1998) 'Assessment and Classroom Learning' *in Assessment in Education 5, 1*

Biggs J.B.

(1988) 'The role of Metacognition in Enhancing Learning' *in Australian Journal of Education 32, 2* pp 127-138

Dillon J.T.

(1994) *Using Discussion in Classrooms* Buckingham: Open University Press

Edwards A.D. & Westgate D.P.G.

(1994) (2nd edition) *Investigating Classroom Talk* London: The Falmer Press

Gipps C.

(1994) *Beyond Testing: Towards a Theory of Educational Assessment* London: The Falmer Press

Mercer N.

(2000) *Words and Minds: How We Use Language to Think Together* London: Routledge

Thinking Through Primary Teaching

2
Introducing the Strategies

'Since the concrete denotes thinking applied to activities for the sake of dealing with difficulties that present themselves practically, 'begin with the concrete' signifies that we should, at the outset of any new experience in learning, make much of what is already familiar, and if possible connect the new topics and principles with the pursuit of an end in some active occupation.'

John Dewey *How We Think (1933)*

SECTION 1 STRATEGIES

2 Introducing the Strategies

The Strategies in this Section are easy to use as they stand and can apply to a range of classrooms and subjects across the curriculum. They offer starting points to try out the activities and the ideas behind them. Each Strategy is described, then specific examples are presented of how it has been used and developed in a particular context. Although these contexts are in specific classrooms with particular age groups of pupils, the activities in this Section are adaptable for pupils of different ages.

Odd One Out

Odd One Out is a versatile Strategy and a good place to start. It can easily be applied and developed in different subjects and with different ages of learners. The Strategy helps to develop an understanding of **key concepts** and **vocabulary** in the subjects of the curriculum.

Exemplar 1	Odd Numbers (Year 3)
Exemplar 2	Odd Animals (Years 1 - 2)

> **Odd One Out** helps teachers assess and develop key concepts and vocabulary.

Fortune Lines and Living Graphs

These related Strategies help pupils to engage with texts and ideas more deeply. The tasks are supported by the visual structure of the graphs or charts that they are based on and by segmenting the text into manageable chunks. They require the use of listening and negotiating skills as well as inference and reasoning.

Exemplar 1	Wild Thing! (Year 2)
Exemplar 2	Busy Road! (Year 3)
Exemplar 3	Eureka! (Year 5)

> **Fortune Lines** and **Living Graphs** develop understanding of text through their visual structures.

Mysteries

In many ways **Mysteries** can build on the skills developed through **Fortune Lines** and **Living Graphs**. They use pieces of paper or card with short pieces of text that can be easily moved on a tabletop. However, they are more demanding in terms of literacy skills: they use pieces of text; successful **Mystery** solvers need to listen to each other, exchange ideas and collaborate effectively.

Exemplar 1	Will Hugh get to the church on time? (Year 6)
Exemplar 2	London's Burning! (Year 2)

> **Mysteries** require collaboration and discussion to develop classification skills and the ability to relate ideas.

Writing Frames

Writing frames are widely recognised as an effective tool to develop writing skills. They can also be used explicitly to support pupils' thinking and understanding of the writing process and different genres of written language. This can be in any subject that requires extended writing. **Writing frames** can also be used to support learners more widely by involving them in identifying how the structure of the **Writing frames** has helped, by breaking down the task into smaller chunks and by developing their understanding of the writing process.

Exemplar 1	For or against? (Year 4)
Exemplar 2	Life Cycle (Year 2)

> **Writing Frames** can be used to develop understanding of different genres of writing as well as specific skills.

Using the Exemplars

We have used the term **Exemplar** in its sense of a model. The Strategies are intended to be flexible in their use in the classroom. Each has been tried out in classrooms by teachers and members of the Thinking Skills Research Centre. They have been used in a range of contexts and schools, from small rural first schools to large suburban primaries and inner city schools. These Exemplars are not recipes however. To try them out you will need to use your professional judgement to adapt them to your own particular circumstances and contexts.

Each Strategy has a **Rationale** providing an overview of the aims and the potential value in pupils' learning. The Strategy is explained in terms of its key features and its focus. Some of the advantages of adopting this approach are outlined. We have not included the theoretical basis and the research underpinning our work in these sections, though these may be explored though the notes in the margins, suggestions for further reading at the end of each chapter, the detailed analysis of the links between teaching thinking and the research on effective teaching in *Chapter 11* and the suggestions for further reading at the end of the book.

The **Procedure** gives an overall picture of the steps required to get started.

Each Exemplar is provided with a brief description of **prior experience** which helps the reader to make sense of the choices the teacher(s) made in using a particular Strategy. However, use of the Strategies is not tied to these particular circumstances. Each teacher will assess specific curriculum knowledge, and develop collaborative working according to the circumstances.

A description of the organisation of the class follows. Some activities or parts of activities lend themselves to **whole class teaching**. Other parts of activities are best handled through **small group work**. Particular aspects of the Strategies are highlighted in the **plenary**.

Development describes how the activity was built upon. Most of the Strategies can be delivered as single activities, though the teachers we have worked with have usually developed their use over a series of lessons. The particular teaching emphasis therefore changes as the Strategies evolve. This section explains some of the teachers' thinking about this.

Further ideas offers suggestions for wider application of the Strategy for other age groups or curriculum subjects. This section also draws on the experience of other teachers who have used the Strategy.

The Exemplars are numbered within the Chapters. Each Chapter deals with a Strategy. *Exemplar 1* is therefore the first one for that particular Strategy. The accompanying *Resource sheets* are numbered in the same way, so *Resource 1* is the first *Resource* for that Strategy. Each page is headed with the name of the Chapter, the name of the Strategy, the name of the Exemplar and the number of the Resource where appropriate.

Thinking Through Primary Teaching

3
Odd One Out

'In the normal process of becoming acquainted with subject matter already known to others, even young pupils react in unexpected ways. There is something fresh, something not capable of being fully anticipated by even the most experienced teacher, in the ways they go at the topic, and in the particular ways in which things strike them. Too often all this is brushed aside as irrelevant; pupils are deliberately held to rehearsing material in the exact form in which the older person conceives it. The result is that what is instinctively original in individuality, that which marks off one from another, goes unused and undirected. Teaching then ceases to be an educative process for the teacher. At most he learns simply to improve his existing technique; he does not get new points of view; he fails to experience any intellectual companionship. Hence both teaching and learning tend to become conventional and mechanical with all the nervous strain on both sides therein implied.'

John Dewey *Democracy and Education (1916)*

3 Odd One Out

Rationale

All kinds of games can be an excellent starting point for thinking Strategies. *Kim's Game*, or *Pairs* or memory games are enjoyable ways to develop pupils' engagement with particular ideas and vocabulary for different subjects in the curriculum. Not only do most of these kinds of games involve some thinking but they also develop important social skills through communication and taking turns.

Identifying similarities and differences is the basis for **classification**. **Odd One Out** is a Strategy which supports **classification** and understanding of the **properties** and **defining attributes** of things. Pupils are asked to identify a similarity which distinguishes two items from a third.

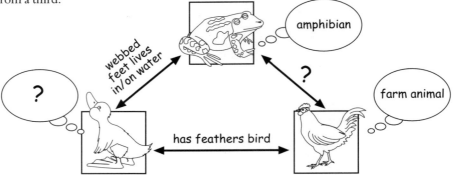

As an activity it can be the basis for whole class work as well as paired or group work. The Strategy can be used across the curriculum, particularly to develop pupils' thinking and use of specific vocabulary. Activities which evoke pupils' use of this kind of vocabulary are powerful diagnostic and formative tools for teachers. This is because the activity frequently provides a window into a child's level of understanding of the ideas involved. The Exemplars in this section are drawn from mathematics and science, though the same idea can be developed in other subjects. The main focus of this Strategy is **classification**.

Some advantages of this Strategy can be summarised as follows:
- key vocabulary is used in a way which develops pupils' understanding of the terminology and its importance in different subjects as they use features to help them classify items in the **Odd One Out** task;
- children start to develop an understanding of connections between items rather than just 'knowing' the properties of individual items;
- it is quick to prepare and to use with a class or group (10-15 minutes can be sufficient);
- it is fun and makes the teacher think as much as the pupils;
- it is relatively easy to make it work and it provides valuable insight into children's thinking;
- it is easy to explain to other teachers.

Procedure

1. Present pupils with three numbers, pictures or names of things, such as animals in science, numerals in mathematics, landscapes in geography.

2. Ask them to identify similarities and differences.

3. Next ask them to choose an **Odd One Out** and give a reason.

4. Encourage them to identify a corresponding similarity for each difference (ie if a square is the odd one out because it is a regular polygon, the other two must be irregular shapes).

5. Encourage a range of answers.

The technique is developed in the two Exemplars below using a triangle format (*Resource 3*) where children select and identify similarities and differences more systematically.

Odd Numbers

Prior experience

The class of Year 3 pupils had experience of describing and identifying simple properties of numbers: odd/even; single digit/two digits; multiple of ten; in the pattern of 3s; doubles; etc. This was developed over the course of a couple of weeks in the oral/mental section of the lesson and in plenaries in the Autumn term. The teacher held up two number cards or wrote them on a flip chart and asked for *'same'* and *'different'* properties. (NB there is potential confusion between 'difference' and 'different' which needs to be made explicit at some point.) This was extended by asking children for other numbers which might go with either of these starting numbers and to state why it is the same or different. (eg, having chosen 3 and 8, 5 is similar to 3 because it is odd, or 9 is similar to 8 because they are both more than 7). The children found that this was difficult at first and tended to identify differences between two numbers, but not consider the third number.

Whole class

Use a large number grid (you could enlarge photocopiable *Resource 1*). At first the teacher covered up parts of the grid so that only one row or column was visible and asked pupils to identify an **Odd One Out** and to state their reason. After they had played the game a few times a whole grid was used with the class. The pupils were encouraged to say the three numbers that were the same and say why they were different from the fourth. The class had also used target boards as oral/mental activities for numeracy lessons and so the pupils were familiar with the layout of the grid.

Small group work

The teacher also developed this as a small group activity. At first this was with the teacher's support, but over a period of about a month (whilst playing the game in introductions and plenaries) the teacher was able to develop the activity as an independent task which was then reviewed in the plenary. The teacher gave out sets of cards with 4 numbers in a set (you could photocopy *Resource 1* several times and then cut up half with the rows as sets of cards and the rest by making sets from the columns). Pairs of pupils were asked to identify an odd one out and to record their reason. To differentiate the activity the teacher provided some groups of pupils with another set of cards with possible answers on (eg, 6 is the odd one out because 5, 7, and 3 are odd numbers). The teacher found that listening to the pupils as they discussed possible reasons was an excellent window into their thinking.

Plenary

To review properties and potential patterns offered by the different pairs of numbers the teacher also used the activities in some plenary sessions. Emphasising that there was usually more than one solution encouraged the pupils to look for alternative answers.

ICT tip: the grids are easy to produce using tables in *Word* or in a spreadsheet where you can alter the cell size and font.

Print them out as landscape A4 pages and enlarge them on a photocopier to A3 for whole class use.

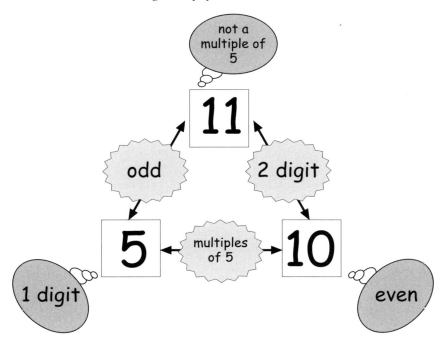

Development

Some pupils found identifying an odd one out difficult. *Resource 3* was used to help them be more systematic in recording what they had found and in finding more than one solution. The idea was to encourage pupils to find different solutions and to identify a corresponding similarity for the remaining pair. If 10 is the odd one out because it is even, then 11 and 5 have a common property of being odd.

Further ideas

Understanding how things are classified in areas of mathematics (or in other subjects) helps learners know what is needed for success.

- Use two or three shapes or other objects to develop mathematical language with younger pupils as a whole class activity focusing on 'same' and 'different'.
- Try cards with key mathematical vocabulary from the *Framework for Mathematics*.
- Develop work on factors and multiples with grids and cards in Key Stage 2 (see *Resource 2* for a Y5 example). Be prepared for surprises as pupils see connections you had not planned.
- Design a grid with quadrilaterals for Y6 to identify defining properties (number of right angles, number of sides of equal length, sides that are parallel, etc). Understanding properties of shapes is a vital part of work in *Shape and Space*.

Possible Odd One Out answers for the target board *(see Resource 1)*

5	6	7	3
11	12	9	13
15	24	11	30
10	50	40	33

Column A:	11 is not a multiple of 5; 5 has only one digit.
Column B:	6 has only one digit/is less than 10; 50 is not a multiple of 3.
Column C:	40 is even; 11 is a palindromic number; nine is a square number.
Column D:	30 is even; 13 is not a multiple of 3.
Row 1:	6 is even; 5, 6, 7 are in a counting sequence.
Row 2:	9 has only one digit/is less than 10; 12 is even; nine is not in a counting sequence.
Row 3:	30 is the only multiple of 10; 11 is not in the pattern of 3s; 11 is prime.
Row 4:	33 is not a multiple of 10; 33 is odd.

Can you think of any others?

Ask for further examples to check understanding.

A key teaching strategy is to ask children to identify another number to go with either the odd one out or the other three. This really checks their knowledge and understanding. For example, in the third row, if 11 is the odd one out because it is not a multiple of three then 4 could go with 11, and 9 could go with the 15, 24 and 30. This can be simplified by suggesting numbers and asking where they would go (at this point it is often easier to use a Venn diagram).

A challenging task is to get pupils to make up their own **Odd One Out** board and see how they manage!

Y3 Odd One Out: target board

3	13	30	33
7	9	11	40
6	12	24	50
5	11	15	10

Y5 Odd One Out: factors and multiples

1	54	36	71
11	55	121	70
100	80	81	25
10	50	90	75

Thinking Through Primary Teaching

Odd One Out: template

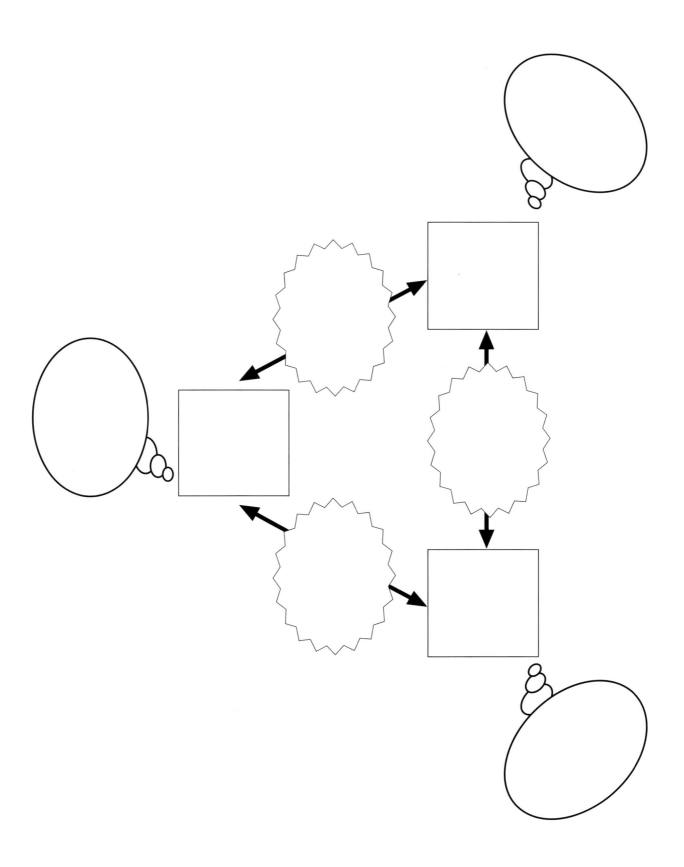

Exemplar 2

Odd Animals

Prior experience

This mixed age class of Year 1 and Year 2 pupils (5 - 7 years) were used to sorting and matching activities generally and particularly for work in science. The teacher had introduced these with a game called *In the Ring*. The children worked in pairs with a sorting hoop and sets of cards with pictures of animals on. She asked them to find animals with four legs and put them in the sorting hoop: 'in the ring'. She then asked questions about the animals 'in the ring' and those 'out of the ring'. She then asked them to take all of the animals out and for other animals to be put in the ring (eg animals that eat grass or plants). The teacher thought that this game in particular has supported the children's success in the **Odd One Out** activities that followed.

Whole class

The activity began with the whole class on the carpet looking at a collection of pictures of animals pinned to a display board. She asked them to choose an odd one out and to give a reason for their choice. She noticed that the children found it easier to identify differences, particularly based on visual features so she encouraged them to articulate and explain what the corresponding similarity was. A version of *Resource 4* was specifically developed to help this.

Small group work

The teacher started with pictures on cards for the younger children in the class (5-6 year olds). She encouraged them to choose two pictures and say that they were either the *'same because...'* or *'different because...'* This was followed up by asking them to choose another picture to make two sets according to one sorting criterion. She felt the children were successful in this because of the experience playing *In the Ring* and explicitly made the link with this activity.

> Making the rules of learning explicit helps some pupils.

The pictures of animals were chosen to focus on particular vocabulary (eg mammals, egg-layers, distinguishing characteristics of insects, etc) and the teacher emphasised to the pupils that they were learning about 'scientific thinking' and that some of the ideas were more important in science that others. When children came up with a feature which was correct, but not relevant to the science curriculum the teacher encouraged them to think of a 'scientific' attribute. This was because some children tended to focus on features, such as colour, which were correct, but not relevant to the science vocabulary the children were learning to use more accurately. Making the purpose of learning clear in this way helped some of the children to be successful.

Development

The teacher developed the Strategy with the older pupils in the class using a grid format. She had used a version of the target boards for **Odd One Out** in a mathematics lesson and created a grid (*see Resource 5*) with pictures of animals for pupils to record one of the odd one out choices they made using the sets of cards.

In the following term, when teaching about materials and their properties, she again used the Strategy in science. The children sorted collections of materials (eg wood, bark, a pencil, a ball-bearing, paper-clip, a toy car, a feather, raw wool, a bone, chalk, glass, a pebble etc) were gathered and a similar process followed, using the *In the Ring* game but providing children with the opportunity to touch and feel the objects.

> Asking pupils to generate further examples is an excellent assessment technique.

The teacher felt that this Strategy gave her an opportunity to understand the children's thinking about the characteristics relevant to **scientific classification**. She felt that one of the most important diagnostic activities was asking children to suggest other animals or objects to go with a set.

Further ideas

A colleague in Key Stage 2 (8 - 11 year olds) in the same school developed activities based on a table format similar to the numeracy target boards (see below).

cat	wolf	lion	tiger
hamster	dog	horse	cow
goldfish	jackal	parrot	butterfly
gerbil	crocodile	dinosaur	lizard

She also used posters of famous paintings and asked her class to identify an **Odd One Out** as an art activity. The stimulus of the examples and the focus of the task enabled the class to produce a wide range of vocabulary, both about the subject matter of the paintings, but also (with some gentle prompting) about the use of colour, line and tone. In this way the **Odd One Out** Approach supported the pupils in using and articulating an appropriate vocabulary for the subject which elicited the accurate use of more demanding vocabulary and supported their understanding of important concepts and ideas in art.

Resource 4   Odd Animals: same or different?

The...

is different because...

....

The......................................and the..

are the same because..

....

Odd Animals: which is the odd one out?   Resource 5

Choose a row or a column. Find something that is the same about two of the animals and something different about the third.

The...

is different because...

....

The..and the...

are the same because...

....

Summary

Odd One Out provides opportunities for pupil to use specific vocabulary in a way that can reveal their understanding of terms that are important for classification. This is part of developing a vocabulary of learning.

Odd One Out aims to develop **classification skills**. It can be used across the curriculum. One of the benefits of using it as a teaching thinking Strategy is that you can make pupils aware of the different way that words are used in different subjects, even for primary pupils (4 - 11 year olds).

Mathematical vocabulary is a good example of this. *Difference* in mathematical language means *numerical* difference and is usually understood by most people in mathematics lessons to mean subtract! However pupils' understanding of the word in other contexts, particularly outside school, is less specific. Saying that the difference between six and nine is one (letter), or that six begins with 's' and nine begins with 'n' can be acceptable answers. Identifying these misunderstandings as reasonable, often logical, errors helps pupils to learn that mathematical or scientific thinking is something that they can get better at, not something that they have to know. Developing a more precise vocabulary and understanding of what is expected within the subjects of the curriculum is part of the focus of teaching thinking Strategies.

Identifying similarities and differences is relatively easy, where children need help is in understanding what makes a good answer in science or in geography. Explicit discussion of what is expected helps many pupils.

Asking pupils to create their own sets or to think of further examples to go with the sets created lets you the teacher see what sort of classification the children can use and to what extent they understand particular vocabulary and ideas.

Odd One Out is a versatile Strategy which can be used across the curriculum. Here are some suggestions to get you started:

- portraits of famous people;
- artefacts from different historical eras;
- characters in traditional tales;
- descriptive words describing settings for a story;
- extracts from poems;
- extracts from different types or genres of writing;
- pictures of landscapes for geographical vocabulary;
- symbols or artefacts in RE;
- statement cards describing causes of events;
- pictures of musical instruments;
- extracts of music (you really need to sample them or have 3 CD players!)

Make sure you use three examples of each. This seems to be the best number of items, particularly as pupils get used to the idea. The application of this Strategy just requires imagination and matching to specific curriculum objectives!

Suggestions for further reading

David Leat's *Thinking Through Geography* (1998, Chris Kington Publishing) explains how this Strategy was developed by a group of secondary geography teachers.

The ideas underpinning the Strategy owe much to George Kelly's personal construct psychology (*The Psychology of Personal Constructs*, Volumes 1 and 2, 1955) where a person's underlying thinking is elicited more systematically. Three statements or ideas are used to expose concepts or 'constructs'. Individuals are asked to link two words or ideas in a way that distinguishes them from the third. For example, banana, lemon and orange might elicit the word 'yellow' linking banana and lemon, or 'citrus', linking lemon and orange. In **Odd One Out** these ideas are elicited in a class for open discussion and modelling of thinking. (The television programme *Have I got News For You* may also have had an influence!)

4

Fortune Lines
and Living Graphs

'If the physical things used in teaching number or geography
or anything else do not leave the mind illuminated with
recognition of a meaning beyond themselves, the instruction
that uses them is as abstruse as that which doles out ready-
made definitions and rules, for it distracts attention from ideas
to mere physical excitations.'

John Dewey *How we Think (1933)*

4 Fortune Lines and Living Graphs

Rationale

The visual structure of the task underpinning these Strategies helps pupils to consider small pieces of information in relation to two key ideas (represented by the axes on the graphs).

These two related Strategies encourage pupils to interpret information and organise it using a familiar visual structure – a graph.

Both Strategies are designed to encourage pupils to consider two aspects of the information at the same time. One of these is usually chronological – the temporal sequence of the events – the other depends on the context chosen for the activity. In the process pupils have to practise and develop crucial skills:

- interpreting information;
- sequencing;
- making links between different pieces of information;
- relating information to two frames or key ideas (the axes of the graph);
- organising information;
- checking and refining;
- explaining;
- justifying.

The Strategy aims to get pupils engaged with text more deeply than by reading a page and answering comprehension questions. It is also challenging in that pupils have to make decisions about the relevance and weight they give to different pieces of information. It is an essential aspect of this Strategy that the information is given to them in small chunks on separate pieces of paper which they can move around on the tables in front of them.

In terms of the National Literacy Strategy used in England, **Fortune Lines** and **Living Graphs** can bridge between sentence and text level work.

The main ideas addressed by **Fortune Lines** and **Living Graphs** are **sequencing** (which usually provides one of the organising features of the **Fortune Line** or **Living Graph**) and **interpreting information** – where pupils have to interpret statements and place them on the graph. They are therefore particularly powerful for supporting humanities subjects such as history, geography and RE as well as appropriate for developing essential literacy and numeracy skills. The pupils are usually motivated by the structure of the task. Working in a pair or small group encourages collaboration and discussion: it is their opinions and reasons that count.

Observing this process and listening to the children as they discuss, put in a sequence, then arrange the pieces of paper on the **Fortune Line** or **Living Graph** is a powerful tool to understand children's thinking.

A **Fortune Line** is usually focused on the experiences or fortunes of a central character or characters. This character can be real or fictional, the only requirement is that they undergo changes in their fortune over time.

A **Living Graph** uses the same basic structure of a graph or chart plus statements on small pieces of card or paper. Again the pupils have to place these statements in an appropriate position on the graph. In **Living Graphs** the nature of the chart can vary. It might be a block or line graph. Pupils might need to be able to interpret the numerical information, or may simply be using the overall shape of the graph.

Both Strategies need some statements which are ambiguous or which require some interpretation. This ensures that the discussion focuses on interpreting the statements.

In brief the advantages and disadvantages of the Strategies are:

- pupils read and discuss short pieces of text with greater engagement;
- they relate these pieces of text to two key ideas (represented by the axes on the **Living Graph** or **Fortune Line**) and draw on their own understanding and experience;
- the Strategy is relatively straightforward to plan, prepare and manage;
- it is easy to develop levels of simplification and challenge.

Procedure

These Strategies require some preparation and planning to work out the range and level of difficulty of the statements.

1. Give pupils a set of cut-out statements and ask to relate them to a prepared graph.

2. Have them work in pairs, or small groups, to identify where on the **Fortune Line** or **Living Graph** the statements fit best.

3. Encourage them to move the pieces of paper around to find the best point on the graph.

4. Start with just three or four short statements for younger children.

5. Develop the activity by including a greater range of statements where either the sequencing is more challenging or assigning the position is more difficult.

Exemplar 1

Wild Thing!

This **Fortune Line** activity is based on *Where the Wild Things Are*, by Maurice Sendak. Pupils in a Year 2 class were given statements from the story *(Resource 1)* and asked to put them in order and then decide whether Max would be feeling happy or sad. It has been adapted for other stories and has been used by teachers as a literacy hour activity as well as in other subjects across the curriculum.

Prior experience

The pupils were used to sequencing pieces of text to help re-tell a familiar story. They also had experience of working in pairs on a piece of work where there was only one finished product. The teacher uses paired games as a regular activity in mathematics teaching which she feels supports the pupils' working together. They had undertaken a similar activity as a class using sentences and pictures from *Willy the Champ*, by Anthony Browne, to plot how Willy felt on a similar **Fortune Line** with a simple smiley face scale during the previous week.

Small group work

Some children were able to work independently, discussing the statements and placing them on the smiley graph *(Resource 2)*. When they had completed the activity they stuck them in place. The teacher worked with a group of children to help them sequence the statements first then discussed with the group how Max would be feeling. These children each had their own set of statements and graph. The teacher knew that it had been especially valuable for one child in particular to articulate her own experience of how it feels to be told off in this small group. She felt that the group she worked with needed extra support in reading and re-reading the statements which they might not have had working in pairs.

Plenary

The teacher chose three of the children to explain their finished work to the class, who contributed their own opinions about Max's feelings through the story. She skilfully elicited ideas based on the information in the text as justification for positioning on the **Fortune Line**. In addition she praised particular pairs of pupils for the way in which they had listened to each other and agreed as well as for the way they had read the statements carefully. This provided pupils with feedback about the process of working as well as the particular curriculum objectives in English for sequencing and interpreting text for the outcomes of the task.

Development

The teacher developed the **Fortune Line** activity using characters from traditional stories and tales. This helped the children to understand the way stories are structured, particularly by plotting the fortune of the heroine or hero and the chief villain. This also provided a springboard to discuss how the fortunes of the characters interact with each other. Some children experimented with planning their own stories using a **Fortune Line**.

Further ideas

It is possible to support the activity for some pupils by making the sequencing part of the task easier. You can number some of the statements so that there is no sequencing involved. To provide more of a challenge add more statements (though be careful as it becomes hard to cope with too many pieces of paper on the graph). Another possible extension is to ask pupils to identify other sentences from the text or book that could be added to the graph.

Versions of this Strategy have been used particularly in English and history to help pupils develop their understanding of fictional characters and develop empathy with historical figures.

> ICT tip: the statements are easy to create with a word processor or DTP program. Make a graph with the page set-up set to landscape then enlarge it to A3 to give pupils more space to move the statements around.

> **Fortune Lines** chart the changes in a person's fortune over time. This can be a fictional character, such as Max, or an historical one, such as Sir Walter Raleigh.

Statements for 'Wild Thing!': Max's Fortune Line

Max made mischief of one kind and another.	He was sent to bed without eating anything.
He found his supper waiting for him.	He sailed off through night and day.
Max stepped into his private boat and said goodbye.	They made him king of all the wild things.
The wild things roared their terrible roars and gnashed their terrible teeth.	But Max was lonely.

To make the task more challenging, consider adding more statements to the set. You may then need to offer additional support in sequencing the statements first, then ask children to transfer them to the feelings graph. You may want to enlarge the example graph *(Resource 2)* to A3.

Let the wild rumpus begin!	And it was still hot!

How did Max feel?

End

Middle

Beginning

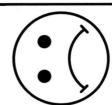

Thinking Through Primary Teaching

Busy Road

This **Living Graph** activity asks pupils to relate statements about people and their work to a chart of the amount of traffic passing the school gates. The value of the Strategy is in giving pupils time to articulate and discuss their thinking about short pieces of text which they relate to the graph. This gives them experience in identifying how realistic statements relate to the visual structure of a chart. As they explain and justify their reasons it provides opportunities for the teacher or their peers to identify and address any misinterpretations or misunderstandings.

> **Living Graphs** relate short statements based on different people's experiences to a chart based on numerical information.

Prior experience

The pupils in this Year 3 class had experience of reading information from bar charts and were generally confident in explaining what a particular bar indicated. They had also undertaken a **Fortune Line** activity in literacy based on the contrasting fortunes of Little Red Riding Hood and the Wolf.

Whole class

The teacher introduced the graph to the whole class using an enlarged version. He discussed the graph first in general terms relating it to everyday language such as the busiest time and the quietest time. He read out two of the statements from the set for discussion and asked where they should be placed. One of these had a clear point on the graph where it should be placed, based on the time mentioned, the other was more ambiguous. He stressed the importance of discussing the statements and everyone being able to explain the reason for their position on the graph.

> The emphasis is on developing skills in interpretation, explanation and on justifying their reasoning.

Small group work

Pupils worked in pairs or threes. From his evaluation of the earlier **Fortune Line** activity that the class had undertaken the teacher wanted to make sure that the children did not see it as a task with a single solution. As he went round the groups he stopped the class and described what some of the pairs were doing, asking them explain their reasoning and therefore model their thinking to the class. Two or three groups finished the task quickly so the teacher asked them to write some statements of their own to add to the graph.

Plenary

In the plenary the teacher focused on discussing, or **debriefing** both the process of the task (eg *'What was hard about working together? How did you make sure your partner agreed?'*) and the content and quality of their reasoning (eg *'Did you think of any other places it could have gone? Why did you think this was better?'*). The teacher was pleased that a number of children had realised that the busiest times outside the school were at the beginning and end of the school day. He used the opportunity to discuss the importance of being careful when arriving and going home. At the end of the lesson one child commented *'It's us that make it busy, it's us that make it dangerous'.*

> In the debriefing it is important to focus on both the process of learning as well as the curriculum content of what has been learned.

Possible development

It is possible to support the activity for some pupils by making the clues clearer, such as by adding words or phrases about times of day. The disadvantage of this is that it tends to close down the discussion. An important part of the task is the talking that goes with justifying where the statements should be placed. This means that some of the statements need to be ambiguous or at least need to be open to interpretation. Another possible development is to ask pupils to identify other statements, as the teacher did in this example, which can be added to the graph.

Further ideas

Living Graphs have been used particularly in history, geography and science to help pupils to interpret and understand information in graphs and charts. Relating the visual and numerical data represented in a chart or graph to pieces of text describing peoples' experiences seems to be a powerful Strategy to develop understanding.

Resource 3   Statements for 'Busy Road' Living Graph

Mrs Nixon, the headteacher, drives her car into the school car park.	Mr Jordan drops Lee, David and Ellie at the school gate.
PC Smith drives home from nightshift.	Mrs Al-Asadi collects Jamal and Jemma from school.
A bus drives past the school. It is full of people going to work.	At 2 o'clock, a van driver delivers some paper to the school.
Mrs Scott, the teaching assistant, leaves the car park to go home.	Ms Peters, who delivers the post, drives home for her lunch.

To make the task more challenging, consider adding more statements. These might include statements that have no clear time clues. You may then need to offer additional support in interpreting the statements first, then ask children to transfer them to the **Living Graph**. You may also want to enlarge *Resource 4* on to A3 paper.

Caspar, the caretaker's cat, crosses the road.	Mr Garner, the lollipop man puts on his coat and collects his stick.
Miss Finlay, the doctor, drives to see Mr Miller who is ill.	A van goes to Mrs Wilson's house to deliver some flowers for her birthday.

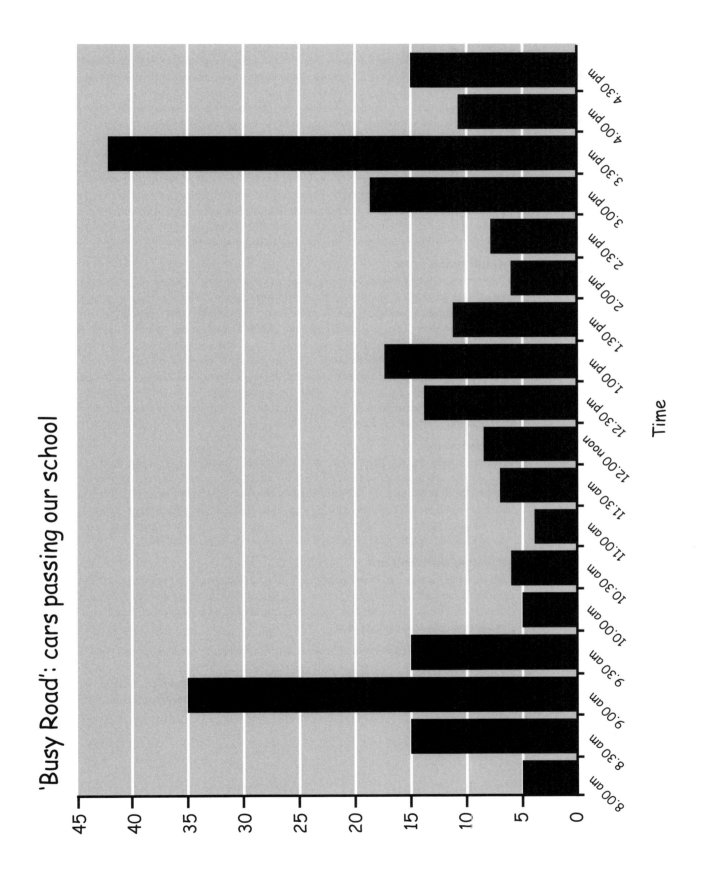

'Busy Road': cars passing our school

Number of cars

Time

Exemplar 3

ICT tip: A simple graph is easy to create in desk-top publishing software such as *Apple Works* or *Microsoft Publisher*. Draw the two axes with the straight line tool and label them with text boxes. More complex charts are easy to create from a spreadsheet program as you can alter the numbers to make the graph more precise. Most programs have on-screen help, such as the 'chart wizard' in Microsoft's *Excel*.

Eureka!

This **Living Graph** activity is based on *Mr Archimedes' Bath*, by Pamela Allen. Pupils in a Year 5 (9 - 10 year olds) class were given statements from the story and asked to place them on the line graph of water level in his bath.

Prior experience

The pupils knew the story from science work and were starting to draw and interpret line graphs as part of their work in organising and interpreting data in mathematics. They also had experience of working together in small 'teams' of five or six pupils. At first these had been grouped according to friendship preferences. The teacher had then steadily mixed the groups so that the pupils were used to working with a range of other pupils.

Whole class

The teacher introduced the line graph using a large version drawn on a flip-chart. She drew attention to the axes and the labels 'full' and 'empty' then asked them to describe, in general terms what they thought might be happening at different points on the line. She reminded them of the story, but did not read it out as she thought they might remember the sequence of the story rather than focusing on the graph. She asked individuals to summarise the plot, identify Mr Archimedes' problem and what he had discovered.

Small group work

Pupils then worked initially in small groups of two or three. Each group had a copy of the graph and the statements photocopied onto thin card and cut out (*Resource 6*). They were asked to take it in turns to read out a statement and identify where it might go on the line graph (*Resource 5*). They put the letter from each statement at the point on the graph where they thought it fitted best. Once most small groups had completed this they were asked to reach agreement as a team and come up with a solution. They were used to one member of the group acting as a team leader to record the team's decisions. Each team discussed what they had decided as a group to record on a team chart. The teacher stopped the class occasionally to praise groups or team leaders for the way that they managed the feedback process and reaching a consensus.

Plenary

In the plenary the teacher took feedback from the 'team leaders' about their choices for placing the statements. She drew attention to where a statement referred to a *point* on the line graph (for example statement I) or a *section* of the line (such as statement E). Then she asked each group to identify where working as a group had been helpful. She gave them a further few minutes to discuss this in small groups then in their teams. Some groups were then called on to explain how they had changed their minds in the team discussion.

Possible development

The teacher was keen to develop the small group and team method of working. She felt that the feedback and 'feed-forward' was an effective way of allowing pupils to reflect and change their minds easily. The focus on effective group work had an impact on discussion in other areas which she felt was beneficial.

In terms of her objectives in mathematics she thought that most of the pupils were confident in interpreting the line graph and planned further activities which focused on the interpretation and explanation of data rather than the skills of drawing the graph. She felt that she could now apply the Strategy more widely across the curriculum, particularly in history and geography.

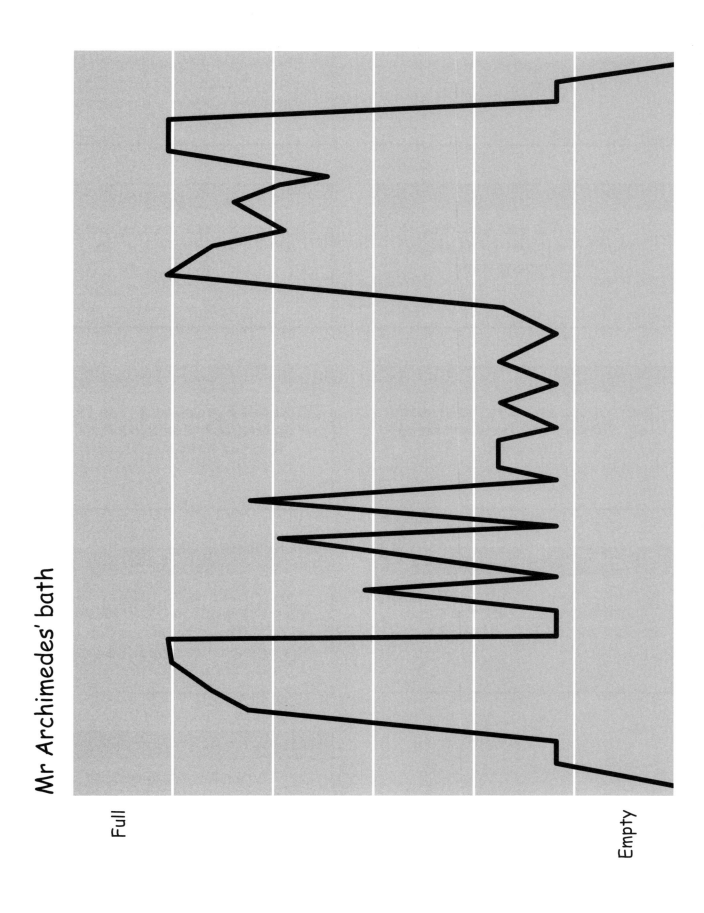

Mr Archimedes' bath

Full

Empty

Statements for 'Eureka' Living Graph

A

Mr Archimedes got so excited that he jumped in and out, in and out to make the water go up and down.

E

The friends had so much fun that night, jumping in and out, making the water go up and down, that they made more mess than ever before.

B

'Maybe it is you, Kangaroo. You stay out and we shall see if it happens again.'

F

'Now let's see what happens when you are left out, Goat.'

C

'Get out and stay out,' he shouted at Wombat. But the same thing happened.

G

'EUREKA! I've found it, I've found it!' he shouted. 'Jump in everyone!' And the bath overflowed.

D

He climbed out, and the water fell until there was just the same amount Mr Archimedes had put in.

H

Mr Archimedes decided to find out. He put just a little water in the bath, as he always did, and this time he measured the depth.

I

When Mr Archimedes measured it again the water had gone down. Mr Archimedes was puzzled.

Summary

Fortune Lines and **Living Graphs** are designed to develop pupils' understanding of the meaning of the different ways that we represent information. Both Strategies break a text up into small pieces or 'chunks' that they can relate to a particular visual frame or structure.

The visual structure of the graph seems to help pupils interpret the information more easily and perhaps more meaningfully. Having the chunks of text on small pieces of card or paper helps them to engage with the text systematically. The pieces of card or paper can be moved around easily, or put aside and dealt with later. This flexibility can be important and can help the teacher to support pupils in choosing easy and then more difficult statements to discuss.

The Strategies can be used across the curriculum and work well in both real and fictional contexts.

Suggestions for further reading

Fortune Lines are described in *Probing Understanding* by Richard White & Richard Gunstone (1992, Falmer Press ISBN 0-75070-048-3). Their examples of introducing this technique through traditional rhymes and tales are particularly accessible and helpful.

David Leat's *Thinking Through Geography* (1999, Chris Kington Publishing) has a section on **Living Graphs**.

Peter Fisher's 'Analysing Anne Frank: a case study in the teaching of thinking skills' in *Teaching History 95*, May 1999 pp 24 -31. (Historical Association. ISSN 0040 0610) describes a **Fortune Line** activity based on extracts from her famous diary.

Peter Fisher has also edited *Thinking Through History* (2001, Chris Kington Publishing) which describes how these two Strategies, amongst others, have been applied by Key Stage 3 (11 - 16) history teachers. Viv Baumfield has edited *Thinking Through RE* (2001, Chris Kington Publishing) which also exemplifies these and other teaching thinking Strategies.

Thinking Through Primary Teaching

5
Mysteries

'The second consideration [about education] depends on relations
given in certain situations - relations accidental to it, which
consequently are not necessary and admit of infinite variety.
Thus, one education may be practicable in Switzerland and
not in France... The greater or lesser facility of execution depends
on countless circumstances that are impossible to determine
otherwise than in a particular application of the method to
this or that country, to this or that place.'

Jean-Jacques Rousseau   *Preface to Emile (1762)*

5 Mysteries

Rationale

Mysteries are particularly powerful Strategies when working with older pupils. Our experience suggests that they can transform the teaching and learning process. The work described here grew out of development of this Strategy by David Leat. His work (on the Kobe earthquake) was used in the Schools Curriculum Assessment Authority (SCAA) *Key Stage 3 Optional Tasks and Tests in Geography* and it is also demonstrated on the *Key Stage3 Literacy* video.

The Strategy hooks pupils in with the central question and the pieces of narrative describing people and their activities. It is designed to encourage pupils to deal with ambiguity through addressing a question which has no single correct answer and where they are not even sure what information is relevant – like in real life. In the process they have to practise and develop crucial skills:

- sorting relevant information from irrelevant information;
- interpreting information;
- making links between different pieces of information;
- speculating to form hypotheses;
- checking and refining;
- explaining;
- justifying.

> **Mysteries** are a demanding Strategy – for pupils and teachers.

The Strategy aims to engage pupils more deeply with a piece of text than reading a page and answering comprehension questions. It challenges pupils to make decisions about the relevance and weight they give to different pieces of information. One essential aspect of this is that the information is given to pupils in chunks on separate pieces of paper which they can move around on the tables in front of them.

> **Mysteries** support classification skills as well as inference, deduction and hypothesising.

The main ideas addressed by **Mysteries** are **classification** (which underpins the way they make connections), **hypothesising** or **generating theories** and **cause and effect**. **Mysteries** are particularly powerful in supporting humanities subjects such as history, geography and RE as well as supporting essential speaking, listening and literacy skills.

Pupils are *engaged* by the curiosity of the **Mystery** and working as a group encourages **collaboration** and **discussion**.

Observing the process and listening to the children as they discuss and classify, then organise and arrange the information on the pieces of paper is a powerful tool for developing teachers' diagnostic and formative assessment skills.

Debriefing the session is challenging and requires the teacher to make complex judgements whether to consolidate or extend key points; what and how to **bridge** or connect ideas; how much emphasis should be placed on reviewing and developing content or curriculum objectives; how much the process of doing the activity and the process of learning can be evaluated.

Procedure

1. Introduce a central question: the **Mystery**.

2. Present the pupils with 15 - 30 pieces of information on small cards: **the clues**.

   These cards should include a range of statements (depending on the **Mystery**), but will normally include the following:
   - background factors;
   - trigger events;
   - red herrings (you need to warn pupils if you use these) or less significant factors;
   - factual information about the characters and setting;
   - opinions.

3. Support the pupils in becoming familiar with the information.

   This might be by getting each person in the group to read out a card in turn. The advantage of cards is that they can be moved around. You might encourage pupils to sort them into sets and come up with a label for the sets.

   This part of the process requires a high level of collaboration which the pupils need to be prepared for in advance. Alternatively you can develop collaborative skills the first time you use this Strategy.

4. Encourage groups to come up with a tentative solution.

5. Ask for opinions from other groups to see if this helps change their minds.

6. Debrief the process of working together as well as the 'solutions' to the task.

Exemplar 1

Will Hugh get to the church on time?

Prior experience

This class of Year 6 pupils (10 - 11 year olds) had just finished their National Curriculum tests in the summer term. They were used to working in groups and had effective collaborative skills. The teacher planned the activity as a challenging task which would support their learning as well as engaging their enthusiasm. The teacher also knew that the history and geography departments in the secondary school used this Strategy so hoped that the debriefing would help the children to see how the Strategy can help their learning.

Whole class

The teacher introduced the activity to the whole class with a short video clip from the beginning of 'Four Weddings and a Funeral' (edited for expletives!). He then introduced the activity as a mathematical challenge and explained what resources were available to them. These included driving atlases, large maps of the UK and some driving 'ready-reckoners'.

> Red herrings need flagging up with Key Stage 2 pupils. Many are used to having to use *all* of the information given.

He also explained how he wanted them to work and that each group needed to be able to explain their answer. The pupils were used to working in mixed ability groups (largely based on friendship) of different sizes for different activities. He passed out envelopes with sets of the clues (*Resource 1*) for each group and warned them that there were some 'red herrings' in the collection.

Small group work

> Providing the class with feedback during group work helps to keep the class working together.

The pupils worked in groups of four or five. The groups used a range of strategies to become familiar with the information. Some took it in turns to read out all of the cards before beginning any of the sorting, others started to categorise the information as they read through them. The teacher stopped the groups for a short period of time and asked three of the groups to explain how they were working and what initial categories they were using. He then sat

> Identifying categories develops metacognitive awareness.

with one of the groups that he felt needed support with this stage of the activity. He encouraged them to adopt one of the strategies mentioned by another group and to find all of the statements which referred to places on the journey. He suggested that they lay these out on a large blank UK map (*Resource 2* – enlarged to A3). This helped them to realise that one of the clues (about the M4/M5) was a red herring. He praised them clearly for this, so that

> Observing and listening then interacting and mediating is formative assessment.

other groups would notice, and asked the class if they had found any other red herrings to ensure that none of the groups spent too much time working out the wrong journey.

> The most effective strategies are made available to everyone in the class.

The teacher observed that one of the groups of pupils who used the outline map of the UK had started to sketch in sections of the journey with times and distances and encouraged other groups to use the same strategy. Not all did so, one successful group laid the statements about places in geographical sequence and the general statements about travelling in a set above. They then worked out a time-line of the journey from London to Inverness.

Plenary

As the groups finished and came up with a solution the teacher asked each group to appoint a presenter to explain their solution to the class. He drew out the differences between the groups in their ways of working as a key part of the debriefing. Some time was spent checking on time and distance calculations as a couple of the groups had made some mathematical errors.

In this discussion one pupil suggested that it would be better to fly to Inverness so the teacher asked them to research the journey by coach, train and air to see if there was a better solution.

Development

The activity was so popular with the class that the teacher used the Strategy several more times before the end of the year. Some groups of pupils were easily able to use the clues to discuss and come up with solutions, others benefited from more structured suggestions for sorting and organising the information. The transformation of text into chunks which can then be manipulated offers a more visual and practical task which is an important Strategy for effective teaching.

Statements for:
Will Hugh get to the church on time?

Friday June 9th 8.30am, a friend, Kate, rings Hugh at home in London inviting him to her wedding.

There are terrible traffic jams on the M4 and M5 which cause delays of up to two hours on the morning of Friday June 9th.

The wedding is held in a church near Inverness, in Scotland.

It is 870 kms from London to Inverness.

Hugh and Kate share the same birthday, June 21st.

The wedding is at 12.30pm on Saturday 10th June.

Each stop takes about half an hour for petrol and food.

He packs quickly and leaves at 9.00 in the morning.

In three hours of driving Hugh covers about 250 kms (if he is not held up in a traffic jam).

It is OK to drive for about 3 hours at a time before you must stop for some food and petrol and to go to the toilet!

It takes an hour and a half to go the first 30 kms because the traffic in London is so slow.

After nine hours of driving Hugh is very tired and decides to stop in a hotel for the night.

Continued...

Resource 1

...Continued

Statements for:
Will Hugh get to the church on time?

> Hugh has forgotten the name of the church in Inverness. It takes him three-quarters of an hour to find it.

> Breakfast is served in the hotel dining room from 7.00am on weekdays and 7.30am at weekends.

> He leaves after breakfast on Saturday morning.

For a further challenge try this alternative ending...

> On Saturday morning the car won't start.

> It is 15 minutes by taxi to the railway station nearest the hotel.

> The trains leave every 45 minutes starting from 7.30 in the morning.

> It takes 20 minutes in a taxi from Inverness railway station to the church.

> **Internet extension:**
>
> Do you think it would it be easier to go by train for the whole journey? If you have access to a computer with internet access try the on-line rail timetable at Railtrack's website and see if a train journey would be easier. Rail track's site is at: http://www.railtrack.co.uk/index.htm
>
> Click on the 'timetable' link and put in London Kings Cross as the starting station and Inverness for the destination.

> Where is the nearest airport to Inverness? Could Hugh have flown...?

> What about a coach journey?

Scale

| 0 | 1cm | 2cm |
| 0 | 50km | 100km |

ICT tip: the Internet provides a rich source of information for creating **Mysteries**, particularly for history and geography.

Exemplar 2

London's Burning!

Prior experience

The class of Year 2 pupils had undertaken work in literacy and history reading texts and gathering information about the Great Fire of London. They had read extracts from the journals of John Evelyn and Samuel Pepys and written journal accounts of their own. The teacher wanted to finish the unit of work by providing an opportunity for the pupils to use the information they had gathered in a discussion and decided on the **Mystery** format. This was partly so that she could assess how much of the information the pupils had assimilated, but also an opportunity for them to use the information in an engaging context.

She had used **Living Graphs** and **Fortune Lines** in literacy teaching previously and thought that they would be able to tackle a text based activity working in pairs and in threes.

Whole class

The teacher spent some time reviewing the activities and materials that they had completed for this unit of work. She then introduced the **Mystery** and the **clues**. In pairs or threes, the pupils took it in turns to read out the statements to each other. Then she asked a series of questions, asking them to them to find clues relating to the baker, or clues about the fire, or clues about how they fought the fire.

Small group work

Once she felt that they were familiar with the statements she asked them to see if they could make a set of the statements which they though answered the question. At this stage of the activity they worked in their small groups.

Debriefing does not have to happen only in the plenary. It can be used to summarise and focus attention at different stages of the activity.

As the groups sorted their statements she listened to their discussions. She stopped the class on a number of occasions to review and debrief what was happening in the groups with the whole class. At first her focus was on ensuring that the pupils understood the process they were supposed to be following. She praised pupils who were listening well to each other, or who had come up with sets of important statements. This ensured that all of the groups were making progress.

As the activity developed she started to ask the groups what answer they had come up with. At first some children were keen to blame the baker, as the fire had started in his ovens. However another group quickly said that *it wasn't his fault that all the people had died, it was the Council's fault that there wasn't a fire brigade!* A further group countered that the people should not have *built wooden houses so close together*.

She asked them to return to the 'clues' to find the best 'evidence' that they could.

Plenary

Collaborative learning can be developed to form the class into a community of learners.

Each group reported on their views to the class. The teacher encouraged them to explain their reasoning and to listen to the other groups to see where they agreed and where they disagreed. She then spent some time highlighting groups and individuals who had collaborated effectively, or who had listened to each other. She stressed the value of learning from each other. As the session ended one of the pupils commented *'it's like listening to your thinking, only you can see where it isn't right'* !

Who was responsible for the Great Fire of London?

Thomas Farrinor was Baker to King Charles II.

The Baker forgot to turn off his oven.

The Baker said that he thought he had put out his oven, but embers from the fire set light to nearby firewood.

Riverfront warehouses were bursting full of oil, tallow and other combustible goods.

The Baker's maid was the first victim of the Great Fire.

The Baker lived in Pudding Lane.

Most of the houses and buildings were made of wood and many had thatched roofs.

Sparks from the Baker's burning house fell on hay and straw at the Star Inn.

The people tried to put the fire out with buckets of water.

The fire started in Pudding Lane.

Hundreds of rats lived in Pudding Lane.

The buckets were made of wood and leather.

Lots of people spent time saving their things instead of trying to stop the fire spreading.

Houses were pulled down to stop the fire spreading, but wood and rubbish were left lying in the street.

On Wednesday night the wind hushed and the fire burned gently.

The fire began at night when everybody was asleep.

The buildings caught fire very easily.

The strong easterly wind kept the fire burning.

The fire destroyed about four-fifths of the city, or more than 430 acres.

About 13,200 houses, nearly 90 parish churches, and nearly 50 livery company halls were burnt down.

Summary

Mysteries are a challenging thinking skills Strategy which take some time to plan and prepare. However the work required in researching and preparing the clues is worth the investment of time and effort. They are particularly good activities for the teacher to eavesdrop into conversations as the groups discuss their points of view.

Further reading and information

Thinking Through Geography, edited by David Leat, has some examples of **Mysteries** used in geography in secondary schools and an academic article by David Leat and Adam Nichols entitled 'Brains on the table' (in *Assessment in Education 7.1* pp 103-121 2000) explains how much is revealed in the process of sorting the statements. The authors argue strongly that it is important to observe and eavesdrop on these conversations rather than intervening too quickly.

A DfEE video, part of the Key Stage 3 literacy materials, shows a **Mystery** being used (*The National Literacy Strategy Key Stage 3 Conference Pack* DfEE).

There is a wealth of information, pictures and facsimiles of original documents on the World Wide Web. Try a search using one of the major search engines for the theme or unit of work you need.

The history net has information about the Great Fire of London:

http://www.thehistorynet.com/BritishHeritage/articles/1995_text.htm

The inspiration for the mathematical **Mystery** came from a website of maths problems. Thanks are therefore due to *'JK'* and *the 'Wedding in Inverness'* problem posted at:

http://www.ourquestions.com/problems/problems1/inverness.html

6

Writing Frames

'Bitzer,' said Thomas Gradgrind, 'your definition of a horse?'
'Quadruped. Graminivorous. Forty teeth, namely, twenty four
grinders, four eye-teeth, and twelve incisive. Sheds coat in the
spring; in marshy countries sheds hoof too. Hoofs hard, but
requiring to be shod with iron. Age known by marks in mouth'.
Thus (and much more) Bitzer. 'Now girl number twenty,' said
Mr Gradgrind, 'you know what a horse is'.

Charles Dickens *Hard Times (1854)*

6 Writing Frames

Rationale

Writing frames help to develop pupils' skills in writing by structuring their written responses. The **frame** provides this structure with clear sections and verbal prompts. They are particularly helpful for developing skills in non-fiction writing by providing practice in following the structures of different genres of writing and in using the language and vocabulary appropriate to these structures.

Writing frames can help pupils by asking the pupils to select, and think about what they have learnt, by encouraging pupils to re-order information and demonstrate their understanding rather than just copying out text. This enables all pupils to achieve some success at writing, a vital ingredient in improving self-esteem and motivation.

Writing frames can help some pupils in particular by preventing them from being presented with a blank sheet of paper – a particularly daunting experience for those for whom sustained writing is difficult. The **frame** also gives pupils an overview of the writing task by making it clear how much remains to be completed. Writing in primary schools in England has traditionally concentrated on narrative or 'story writing'. **Writing frames** can therefore extend the genres of writing pupils learn to master which prepares them for the types of writing they will need in later stages of their education.

Modelling by the teacher

The teacher models the writing process. This demonstration is an important part of the teaching process.

An important part of the process is the modelling provided by the teacher. A large version of the **writing frame** (or a large electronic version on an interactive whiteboard or data projector) is completed by the teacher. This part of the process is essential. The **frames** are not worksheets to be completed by the pupils unaided.

Implicit use: designing more effective tasks

Writing frames can be used *implicitly* and *explicitly*.

They can be used implicitly and explicitly. When used implicitly the frame is presented as part of the task. At this level they are successful for a variety of reasons. The frame:

- is more inviting than a blank page;
- breaks down the task into a series of steps;
- can offer prompts and specific suggestions for vocabulary to use;
- makes the purpose of writing clear.

Used in this way **writing frames** resemble the Strategies earlier in the book.

Explicit use: developing a vocabulary for learning

Writing frames can also be used *explicitly* as part of the process of learning to write. Used in this way the purpose of the *technique* as well as the task is made clear and understood by the pupils. The teacher uses the modelling process both to demonstrate the skills and to explain her thinking about alternatives. In this way specific targets can be given to pupils about the different parts of the **writing frame**. The teacher reviews with the pupils the *content* of the writing as well as debriefing the *process* of completing the **writing frame** and how she thinks it contributes to making them more successful learners. This final metacognitive step is probably not essential in improving pupils' writing in the shorter term. However we believe it is a vital step in helping children to become successful learners. Used in this way **writing frames** are more like the Approaches described in the *Section 2* of the book.

At this Level **writing frames** help to:

- focus pupils on specific aspects of writing they can improve;
- provide clear targets for improvement;
- make writing seem attainable (rather than something that you are just 'good at' or not);
- develop a metacognitive vocabulary (by talking about learning).

The Strategy is designed to support pupils by providing a **structure** (the sections of the **frame**) and **prompts** (the language used in each of the sections, or **specific vocabulary**. The structure needs to be withdrawn over a period of time, so that the pupils can write independently and effectively without the **frame**.

Procedure

A possible procedure for teaching **writing frames** might be as follows.

1. The teacher demonstrates using large version of the **frame (modelling)**.

2. The teacher and pupils complete a **writing frame** together **(joint construction)**.

3. The pupils use a **writing frame** to complete a task which is supported by the teacher and where the writing is seen as a draft **(scaffolding)**.

4. Group discussion of particular examples to develop peer assessment **(group review)**.

5. Plenary discussion of the types of language appropriate for the genre **(whole class review)**.

6. The genre and its language features are added to pupils' writing repertoire **(independence)**.

7. Debriefing and discussion of how **writing frames** help make the process of writing attainable **(metacognition)**.

It is important that **writing frames** are *always* used within appropriate curriculum work rather than in isolated study skills lessons. In other words, the use of a **writing frame** should arise from the pupils having a *purpose* for undertaking some writing and an appropriate **frame** introduced if needed.

Metacognition can work at two levels.

1. Review of the task helps to develop a specific vocabulary of learning relevant to the skills involved in the task in hand.

2. Reviewing learning as attainable helps to develop a vocabulary for learning and a positive attitude towards learning.

Exemplar 1

For or against?

Prior experience

Developing particular genres of language is now an explicit part of the National Literacy Strategy in England. In Key Stage 1 (5 - 7 year olds) children are expected to be able to write simple instructions and to be able to use impersonal language and descriptions By Year 4 (8 - 9 year olds) pupils are expected to be able to summarise and to use persuasive language and to assemble and sequence points of view in constructing an argument.

This class of Year 4 pupils had used **writing frames** previously to help structure their writing for instructional texts and report writing. However the teacher was keen to develop the attitudes of pupils towards writing more generally and planned a series of activities using **writing frames** for literacy teaching but set in different curriculum contexts.

Whole class

> Writing should be set in a context where the purpose is clear.

A new housing estate was proposed for development on the edge of the small town where the majority of pupils lived. The teacher used an article from the local paper as a stimulus for the class discussion before the writing activity and explained that they were going to send in their writing to the local newspaper in response to the article.

The teacher then modelled writing two lists of advantages and disadvantages and talked about the words used for each.

Small group work

The pupils worked in pairs initially to discuss and plan their ideas. They had a copy of the **writing frame** (*Resource 1*) but were encouraged to make their own notes on scrap paper.

> Providing the class with feedback during group work helps to keep the class working together.

Once she was confident that the pupils knew what was expected she asked them to give examples of the points they had come up with.

Plenary

The teacher made sure she discussed ideas from the pupils that were clear examples of:

- establishing a position **(thesis)**;
- stating a point **(the argument)**;
- developing a point **(elaboration)**;
- summary or restatement of the position **(reiteration)**.

> Talking about your thinking models metacognition.

She then completed a large version of the **writing frame** using a flip-chart. To end the session she spent some time talking about how she had planned the **writing frame** and asked pupils to think about how it had helped them to develop their writing.

Using ICT

Writing continued in the afternoon following the focus on writing as part of the pupils' work in geography. The class had a timetabled session in the school's ICT room and used a prepared template file. She had constructed the outline of the **writing frame** in Microsoft *Word* using the table tools. Then she inserted free-text forms into each of the cells of the table. This had the advantage of only letting the pupils enter text in the appropriate places, and retaining the layout of the page.

Development

Over the course of the next few weeks the class undertook further writing tasks developing their understanding of discussion and persuasive writing (*Resources 2 and 3*). These aimed to support:

- a clear statement of the discussion;
- arguments for and supporting evidence;
- arguments against and supporting evidence;
- a summary and conclusion.

> ICT tip: **writing frames** are easy to create and then adapt using ICT. Use the tables and forms tools to make versions for the pupil to complete on screen.

Each of the tasks was set in a similar context of the local area. The second activity was again based on local news; arguments for and against pedestrianising a shopping street in the centre of the town. The final one was taken from sources of information on the internet, examining arguments for and against drilling for oil in Alaska.

Thinking Through Primary Teaching

In terms of developing literacy, the teacher aimed to develop the pupils' understanding of the genres of argument and discussion. She had clear evidence of work progressing towards this goal.

After the final session she planned an 'awards ceremony' session where she reviewed the development in the pupils' writing using the three **writing frames**. They were each encouraged to identify an aspect of their understanding of argument and discussion that had improved.

> It takes time to develop metacognition and the language of learning.

The teacher felt that the series of tasks had achieved both of her main aims. She felt it had helped pupils' writing and their understanding of argument, discussion and persuasive text in particular. This was partly because the tasks tapped into their opinions and set the writing in a purposeful context. In addition she thought that for some of the pupils the tasks had also helped them see themselves as more successful writers, though this would require further development in the future.

Resource 1   For or against?

Name:	Date:

Title:

The issue is:

Arguments for:	Arguments against:

So I think

This is because

For or against?
Using evidence

Name:	Date:

Title:

The issue is:

Arguments for:	Arguments against:
First point: The evidence for this is	First point: The evidence for this is
Second point: The evidence for this is	Second point: The evidence for this is
Third point: The evidence for this is	Third point: The evidence for this is

My conclusion is

This is because

Resource 3   # For or against?
Looking at both sides of the argument

Name:	Date:

Title:

Some words you might use:

because	I think that	considering
but	I know	in balance
however	one reason is	more important
so	another point is	
this means	the strongest argument	

Arguments for:

Arguments against:

In conclusion:

This is because

Life Cycle

Prior experience

The class of Year 2 pupils (6 - 7 year olds) were accustomed to using a variety of planning sheets and **writing frames** in literacy, but had not used them so extensively in other areas of the curriculum. The children were also just beginning to be able to undertake paired collaborative work and the teacher wanted to develop the pupils' skills in evaluating their own work. In the previous week they had been asked to think up some good words to use in their writing which a partner noted down on scrap paper to help them. They were familiar with the stages in the life of a butterfly and the teacher wanted to use this to develop and assess their understanding of life cycles.

Whole class

The class knew the story of the *The Very Hungry Caterpillar* by Eric Carle well and the teacher used illustrations of this to introduce the task. They were asked to complete and use the sheet (*Resource 1*) to explain the life cycle of a butterfly to one of their friends in preparation for taking it home to explain to their parents. The children were warned that the picture sheet and the dictionary mat contained some words and pictures that they would not need, as well as those that would be useful and that they would therefore have to decide which were the best ones to use in their explanation.

Small group work

The pupils worked individually on their tasks. Some pupils stuck pictures and matched words to complete the circles in the diagram (*Resources 4 and 5*). Others completed sentences in each circle using a dictionary mat with appropriate vocabulary. As they were working they were asked to check that their partner knew what they had to do and to explain where they had got to. Once they had completed this task the teacher stopped the class and highlighted a few examples which exemplified what he had intended. He then asked them to stop and explain their *life cycle* sheet to the person sitting next to them. After this he then asked a series of questions which the '*evaluator*' had to tell the '*author*' whether they understood their explanation and how the *life cycle* sheet helped.

In the final task for the session the children were given another life cycle sheet and asked to choose an animal where they could describe its life cycle. They were asked to draw and write or just write. The children took the butterfly sheets home to explain '*life cycle*' and the teacher kept the final task as a record of their understanding.

> Evaluation of learning is central to teaching thinking. Once pupils can understand why they are doing a task, they can begin to evaluate how well they have accomplished it.

> Teaching for transfer needs to be planned as well as developed as opportunities arise.

Plenary

The teacher chose some of the children to present their own *life cycle* sheets to the class. He encouraged them to explain their thinking about the animal that they had chosen and asked others to comment on the presented work (the pupils were used to doing this and usually made positive critical comments about their peers). The discussion showed that some pupils had clearly understood what was meant by a life cycle (at least within their current understanding), as they could come up with other examples (eg egg, chick, hen, hen lays egg... or egg, tadpole, froglet, frog lays frogspawn), whilst others found describing and articulating this difficult. It was clearly easier for pupils to describe this for animals which had distinct stages (such as insects or amphibians, or even other animals that lay eggs such as reptiles and birds), whereas mammals were more difficult to describe.

He then spent some time talking about why he had arranged the *life cycle* sheet the way it was presented. One child commented '*it's like ... living things have babies and the little babies grow up and have babies*'. The teacher also noted with amusement one of the comments of one of the pupils '*it's called a life cycle coz it goes round and round like a bicycle wheel*'. The teacher thought that the visual structure of the *life cycle* sheet may have helped to support this understanding of *life cycles*.

Development

The idea of a *life cycle* was revisited later in the year when the children completed reports on animals that they researched (*Resource 6*). As they reviewed this activity the teacher reminded them of the earlier work that they had done on *life cycles* and asked them to identify improvements in their knowledge as well as their writing skills.

The teacher also used **writing frames** in science investigations to develop their skills in reporting and recounting what they had done, as well as in explaining their understanding and what they had learned. **Writing frames** were used in other curriculum areas too: comparing historical artefacts and customs; and describing landscapes in geography.

Resource 4   Life Cycle diagram

Date:

Name:

This is the life cycle of a

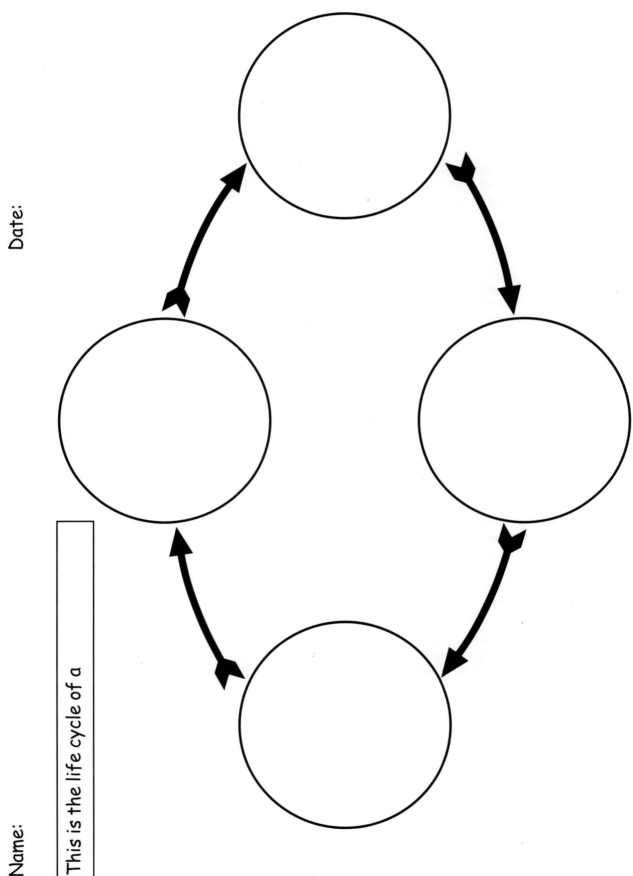

Butterfly life cycle

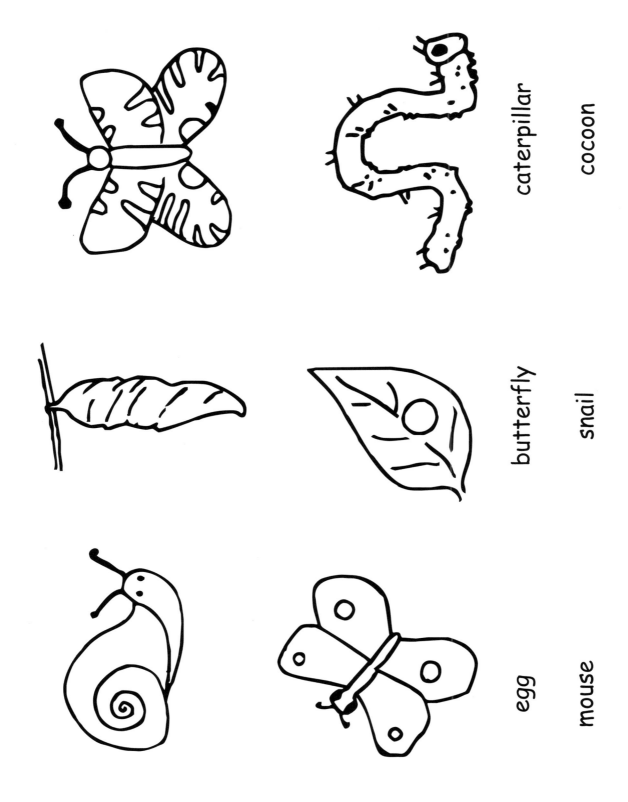

caterpillar

cocoon

butterfly

snail

egg

mouse

Resource 6   Living things report

Name:	Date:

Title:

Definition:

A.. is ....

It is a kind of

Appearance: What does it look like?	It is
Habitat: Where does it live?	It lives
Life cycle: How is it born? How does it change?	It started life as
Food: What does it eat?	

I know that

Summary

Writing frames are an indispensable tool in any teacher's repertoire of activities for developing pupils' writing. They can be used to support the development of specific skills and understanding of the language appropriate to different genres of writing. They can also be used to meet specific curriculum objectives by supporting pupils' writing across the curriculum. These aims are both implicit in the teacher's use of the technique.

In this way, using **writing frames** involves: having a clear purpose for the writing which the pupils can understand; modelling of the writing process by the teacher; and some supported writing (including drafting and improving the writing). The aim is that pupils should be able to use these skills independently in their own writing.

Writing frames can also be used more explicitly to develop understanding of the writing process and how this contributes to the teaching of writing as something attainable. In order to do this, some time needs to be spent with a pupil considering how using the **writing frame** has helped to improve their writing. This metacognitive approach is challenging and not easy to achieve in the short term. However, it is essential that short-term objectives in improving skills (in any area of the curriculum) are not taught to the detriment of a learner's attitude to the whole process of learning. Developing positive attitudes enables learners to see themselves as successful and learning as attainable. It is this disposition towards learning that teaching thinking attempts to create.

> Using **writing frames** for teaching thinking requires metacognition. This can be about the skills involved or curriculum subject content. At the next level pupils begin to evaluate how tasks contribute to their learning. This helps to develop a disposition for learning.

Further reading and information

An essential text for developing understanding of the teaching and learning of writing and literacy more generally is *Extending Literacy* by David Wray & Maureen Lewis (1997). *Chapter 10* looks at *Writing non-fiction* and describes the authors' experience working with teachers to develop pupils' writing using **writing frames**.

Bob Swartz has developed the use of *'graphic organisers'* in the US as frames for writing in *Infusing the teaching of critical and creative thinking into content instruction: a lesson design handbook for the elementary grades.* (Swartz & Parks, 1994. California: Critical Thinking Press & Software).

Alistair Smith's *Accelerated Learning in Practice* (Network Educational Press, 1998) describes an approach to developing pupils' beliefs about themselves as learners using a variety of planning tools, frames, review and evaluation forms.

A good stimulus can make all the difference to an activity. Local newspapers can provide links into the geography and history curriculum. There are surprising sources of information on the Internet – the challenge is in finding them!

7
Developing
the Approaches

'The purpose of the newer movement in education is not to make
things interesting to the child by environing him with a sort of
vaudeville divertisement, with all sorts of spectacular
accompaniments. The aim is to permit the intrinsic wonder and
value which attach to all the realities which lie behind the school
curriculum to come home to the child.'

John Dewey *Education Direct and Indirect (1906)*

SECTION 2 APPROACHES
7 Developing the Approaches

In *Section 1* of the book we looked at the way particular activities can support learning in the primary classroom. These Strategies can be used directly or easily adapted for different age groups and specific curriculum objectives. **Odd One Out** is a good example of this. It can be used as a short diagnostic activity in almost any subject. It can be adapted easily and does not need to involve any discussion of learning to be a valuable teaching tool.

These covered the first two **Levels of use** discussed in the *Introduction*:

Level 1: Using or applying the teaching resources

Level 2: Adaptation and development

In *Section 2* of the book we turn to look at how particular Strategies in teaching thinking can be infused or integrated more closely with some of the subjects in the curriculum, National Strategies for literacy and numeracy, and programmes of study followed in schools in England.

Much of the potential for learning in these activities depends on the connections that are made with pupils' prior learning and the way the learning is assimilated and applied by the pupils. This is often called **transfer** in the research literature on teaching and learning and is an important goal of education. **Transfer** is what enables pupils to connect their learning with other learning in school and with their wider experiences. The teacher aims to support this **transfer** by **bridging** or helping pupils to connect their learning within and between tasks and activities.

In the chapters on **Mysteries** and **Writing Frames** we stressed the importance of making the **process of learning** explicit as well as reviewing the curriculum content or products of tasks. These metacognitive discussions, we argued, are what help to develop positive attitudes and a disposition for learning. Building these bridges between tasks and activities and between curriculum subjects is not easy. It is often hard enough to get all of the pupils to finish an activity, let alone **debrief** it.

Level 3: Debriefing learning and metacognition

This **debriefing of learning** involves the pupils in describing and talking about what they think they have learned and how they have learned it. It is not just a review by the teacher of what she thinks has been taught, though this might form a part of a debriefing discussion. This means setting aside time in lessons, to discuss strategies with pupils. This can structured with:

- **what** did you do?
- **how** did you do it?
- **why** was that effective/a good approach?

For younger pupils, in Reception and Year 1 (4 - 6 year olds) discussion of what they have done is achievable. In Years 2 and 3 children can describe how they did an activity and how they know that they were successful. In Years 4 and 5, pupils will be able to understand why a particular Approach or Strategy was effective and by the end of the primary school it is realistic to expect eleven year olds to know about some approaches to learning which they can use. This might be in terms of specific Strategies or Approaches within a subject like in mathematics or English. In mental calculation, for example, Year 6 pupils should be able to describe how they would tackle a calculation mentally and how a written approach would differ and the advantages and disadvantages of each. Similarly in English they should be able to describe different genres of language and identify some of the typical vocabulary used in specific types. Pupils may also begin to understand where different strategies are useful. **Odd One Out** should help to check understanding of important ideas and concepts. An argumentation **writing frame** provides a structure which they might remember when tackling a practice test question or when writing a letter of complaint for themselves. If the potential for this **transfer** has been developed through **bridging** in lessons, it is more likely the learning will be remembered later. This is the **vocabulary *of* learning** in and across particular subjects mentioned in the *Introduction*.

Developing learners' awareness of learning approaches and strategies is also a possible goal. However, it is not possible to engage in metacognitive analysis every lesson! To begin with it would take too long to do. It would quickly become mind numbing if each activity were to be debriefed and analysed in detail on a daily basis. However, this does not mean that it can't

Level 1 - Application
Level 2 - Adaptation
Level 3 - Metacognition
Level 4 - Infusion

A vocabulary of learning helps start the process of transfer.

be tackled over the course of a few weeks or a term. This is one of the advantages of undertaking *'teaching thinking'*. It enables you to set aside a lesson or two a week to try something different. At first, it is enough of a challenge to undertake a new Strategy. After a while you become familiar with the Strategy, its strengths and weaknesses, and where it fits best for the pupils that you teach. This is when you can start to help pupils to understand their own learning. Developing a **vocabulary *for* learning** and an awareness of their individual strengths and weaknesses requires an even longer term approach.

> Developing a vocabulary for learning takes time.

The teaching thinking Strategies can be used therefore to develop a **vocabulary *of* learning** in and across particular subjects. They also help to develop a **vocabulary *for* learning** as pupils become more familiar with talking about and understanding their own learning and the techniques and approaches that work for them.

Problematic plenaries

Plenaries often seem to be the best place to start. It is the end of the lesson and the ideas and activities should be fresh in their minds. Experience suggests, however, that this might not be the case as plenaries are the most challenging part of any lesson. There are several reasons for this:

- time runs out because the activities overrun;
- pupils know the lesson is about to end and pay less attention;
- you don't want to begin the plenary too early in case there is too much time to fill;
- it is hard to decide whether to consolidate the learning that has taken place, whether to review the particular curriculum objectives or whether to try to **bridge** the learning.

Our suggestion, therefore, is that you try to **bridge** and discuss the learning earlier in lessons as opportunities arise, or remind pupils at the beginning of the next lesson and have a discussion then. If you do want to use the final section of the lesson, to capitalise on what the pupils have just done, plan to start the debriefing as you would a lesson with a particular stimulus or idea to launch this section of the lesson and recapture the pupils' attention.

At the next Level, the teachers in a school work together to develop teaching thinking across age groups and subjects. The Exemplars in the second *Section* of the book illustrate how such infusion has been developed.

Level 4: Total infusion

Infusion is where a whole school approach is required. A group of schools and some individual schools and teachers that we had worked with identified teaching thinking as a priority for staff development, initially over a year. They then extended the work into a second and, in some cases, a third year. This development took place in a time of some turbulence in primary education in England. The implementation of the National Literacy Strategy and the training and implementation of the National Numeracy Strategy overlapped with and influenced the development of the thinking Strategies and activities. This makes interpreting the research data that we collected problematic as changes were also influenced by the national developments. The Exemplars which follow and the description of the integration of thinking skills into English and mathematics are nonetheless valid.

Community of Enquiry

The **Community of Enquiry** is a method of developing pupils' questioning, discussion and reasoning skills. It is based broadly on a Socratic method of dialogue where the class form a community and try to agree answers to questions that they have identified. Once pupils can engage in such discussion the Approach can enhance many of the Strategies in the first *Section* of the book. For example, one of the challenges in **Odd One Out** is to decide what makes a good answer if the Strategy is to be developed into a teaching tool. **Community of Enquiry** can be used as a structure for a plenary discussion. Once the pupils know that they are using the technique to reach consensus, they can use the discussion to agree and disagree with each other. This alters the nature of the language used and the interaction between the teacher and pupils and the pupils with each other.

Exemplar 1   What is Real? (Reception: 4 - 5 year old pupils)

Exemplar 2   Questions, questions, questions (Whole school: 4 - 9 year olds)

Developing mental calculation strategies through metacognition

Developing efficient mental calculation strategies is a key part of the *Framework for Mathematics* used in England. To calculate effectively pupils need both to practice the recall of number facts AND to develop strategies so that they can choose efficient mental methods for different types of calculations. Some individual teachers and a cluster of first schools identified this as a priority for development. They used a *'what? how? why?'* approach to support the pupils' articulation and understanding of a range of strategies.

Exemplar 1   Games and Names

Exemplar 2   Sum Strategies

Using ICT to support thinking and reasoning

ICT offers a range of ways to support pupils' thinking. In these two Exemplars two possibilities are highlighted. In the first, the ICT is used as a catalyst for discussion and thinking which took place away from the computer. In the second case study, software designed to support logical thinking was used and the puzzles and strategies **bridged** to the other subjects in the curriculum.

Exemplar 1   Multimedia Apostrophes

Exemplar 2   Meet the Zoombinis!

8
Creating a Community of Enquiry

'There is more to be learned from the unexpected questions of
children than the discourses of men.'

John Locke *An Essay Concerning Human Understanding (1690)*

8 Creating a Community of Enquiry

Rationale

Creating a **Community of Enquiry** is all about encouraging and supporting genuine discussion and interaction at class level. It was pioneered by Matthew Lipman in the United States as *Philosophy for Children* (P4C) and has been developed in the UK by Robert Fisher in his *Stories for Thinking* and Karen Murris through *Teaching Philosophy with Picture Books*. The roots of the Approach can be traced back to the thinking and writings of John Dewey and his ideas about the role of the individual in their own education and the role of education in shaping society. Some claim the method echoes philosophical enquiry through dialogue dating back to Socrates and the writings of Plato. It is a powerful Approach to developing genuine enquiry skills whilst also supporting pupils' social skills and critical thinking. It complements literacy hour teaching in England by encouraging pupils to ask questions at (and beyond) text level.

Procedure

1. Choose an appropriate text.

2. Share the story (taking turns reading where appropriate though it is important to ensure that all of the pupils can follow the story and do not lose the thread) or listen to a story on tape or watch a video or a presentation on a computer.

3. Ask the pupils to think of questions and record them on a flip chart.

4. Agree questions for discussion, differentiating between more interesting and open questions and more closed or restricting questions.

5. Manage turn-taking in responding to the questions:

   'I agree with Harry because...'

   'I disagree with Hermione because...'

6. Encourage reasoning and interactive discussion.

7. Encourage links with pupils' personal experience and understanding.

> An essential part of the **Community of Enquiry** Approach is in developing genuine listening skills in pupils. They should be encouraged to preface their comments with *'I agree with... because...'* or *'I disagree with ... because...'*

An easy text to get started with is *The True Story of the Three Little Pigs* by Jon Sczieska (1981). This works well at different levels. Young children enjoy the story from the wolf's viewpoint (though very young children can be confused if they are not already familiar with a version of the traditional tale) Older pupils are still engaged by the issues of whether it is reasonable to expect a wolf not to eat a plump pig.

This particular text can generate a range of questions from the factual and implicitly critical *'How can pigs speak?'* to the moral *'Why were the pigs rude?'* as well as the more complex *'If pigs do not like him why do they live next door?'* It has been tried with a range of ages from Key Stage 1 (5 - 7 year olds), to Key Stage 3 (11 - 14 year olds).

The **Community of Enquiry** can support the development of pupils' questioning. In the two case studies which follow we describe how one group of teachers used the Approach to support the development of children's questioning in science; and how a group of schools used it to investigate the types of questions which the children ask in literacy.

What is Real?

A group of teachers in the North East used the Approach advocated by Karen Murris in *Teaching Philosophy with Picture Books* to see if the Approach could improve pupils' questioning skills. None of the teachers had prior experience of teaching thinking, though they had chosen to be part of the project. Science was identified as the focus and in particular the challenging requirements for Key Stage 1 pupils:

> Asking questions is an important part of the requirements of the national curriculum for science.

> *'Pupils should be taught to ask questions (for example, How? Why? What will happen if … ?) and decide how they might find answers to them.'*
>
> National Curriculum for England: Science Key Stage 1, p 16

The teachers attended an introductory day to introduce them to the Approach and then a series of follow-up meetings to feed back to each other their findings in the classroom.

What is Real?

The work took place with a class of Reception children and involved a colleague who usually taught Year 3 (7 - 8 year olds) in observation and support. The story chosen was *The Pig's Wedding* by Helme Heine (one of the texts recommended in *Teaching Philosophy with Picture Books*). In this story Porker Pig and Curlytail are getting married. So that the guests can be dressed for the wedding they paint clothes on themselves. Towards the end of the celebrations it pours with rain and the 'clothes' are washed off.

Whole class work

This particular story was chosen because it fitted in well with one of the themes that the children were studying which was about weddings. The specific learning objective that was identified for the session was that the children would gain some understanding of 'What is Real?' with links to the programmes of study for 'Materials and their properties'. The teacher prepared some questions which she hoped the discussion would cover.

After reading the story the children were asked to think about what they thought was interesting and what they liked best. They were given time to think about their answers before discussing them (the children were used to closing their eyes during 'thinking' time).

After some suggestions as a whole class, children were given the opportunity to discuss their favourite part of the story in pairs, telling one another why it was their favourite part. The teacher then asked specific questions linked to the story. The following is an extract from the transcript.

T: What should you wear at a wedding?

C: I would wear something smart.

T: What are your clothes like?

C: They are made out of material. It's real, it's nice, it's soft. It's nice to wear because it feels nice.

The children touched their own clothing and described it to a friend and compared different types of clothes that people in the class were wearing. The discussion continued until the children were asked if they thought the pig's clothes were real.

C: No, because they were painted clothes. Painted clothes aren't real they're just paint.

T: Can you touch painted clothes?

Class: No!!

T: Can you feel them?

Class: Yes/No

C: Would feel a bit like …. long and dry.

T: Can you change painted clothes? Can you tuck them in?

C: Only if they're painted like that.

T: Can you see real clothes? Can you see painted clothes?

C: Yes, if there's light, if they're both colours and not dark.

T: Can you smell clothes?

C: Yes, if they're real.

C: No.

The children smelled their own clothes

C: Yes.

C: The pig's clothes washed off because they weren't real.

T: How do we know if things are real?

C: If it's hard, it's real.

One of the children illustrated that this is not always true by touching the hair of a boy on the cover of a hardback book and touching her own hair, she then said:

C: We have to think about it. We have to think carefully.

How do we change?

Another Reception teacher in this project used the **Community of Enquiry** Approach to support children's questioning and discussion. Her focus was introducing investigative skills, specifically that:

'pupils should be taught to:

* *ask questions [for example, How? Why? What will happen if ... ?] and decide how they might find answers to them;*
* *use first-hand experience and simple information sources to answer questions;*
* *think about what might happen before deciding what to do'.*

In addition she was looking at life processes and living things (Sc2), *'that animals, including humans, move, feed, grow'*. She chose to use a poem *When I was born* by Karen King as this detailed physical changes from birth to four years. After reading and discussing the poem the teacher channelled the discussion around 'how could we find out what younger children can do?' One child suggested that they could bring a baby in and put it on a ladder to see if it could climb it! The discussion moved on to what kind of toys babies could play with and several children volunteered younger siblings to be experimented on!

In a later lesson (and with considerable parental co-operation) small groups of children from the Reception class observed and recorded what young children could do with a range of toys the class had suggested. When a one month old baby was greeted with cries of *'he can't do anything'* his mother patiently showed how he could grip tightly onto the children's fingers.

Developing the Approach

The teachers in the project recognised the value of the **Community of Enquiry**. The narrative of a story or the structure of a poem provided a context where even young children were confident to ask questions and speculate.

The main tension the teachers found in the project was between using questions recommended in *Teaching Philosophy with Picture Books*, or identifying questions that they wanted to cover, and in encouraging the children to come up with or generate their own questions. In the following case study we changed the Approach to ensure that all of the questions were produced by the children. Although this makes the areas discussed less predictable, it offers a better window into children's thinking. It also shows that, over time, the quality of children's questioning can be developed. One of the classes in the project decided that: *'A good thinking skills question gets you to ask other questions about it.'*

Questions, questions, questions

Four first schools in Northumberland decided to focus on improving children's thinking as part of a local project to raise standards in the local cluster of first, middle and high schools. They wanted to work across Key Stages 1 and 2 and involve children of all abilities. The four schools met together with a Local Education Authority (LEA) adviser, who had some expertise in the infusion of thinking skills into the curriculum, and members of the Thinking Skills Research Centre at the University of Newcastle to plan the project. The aims of the project were to:

- improve the pupils' ability to formulate questions;
- encourage pupils to develop and sustain reasoned argument;
- develop pupils' ability to listen attentively and respond appropriately in discussions;
- promote a disposition that values and respects the opinions of others.

The first challenge was to identify a suitable Approach from the range of existing thinking skills programmes and, after some discussion, it was agreed that, given the need to involve younger children, *Philosophy for Children*, was a good starting point. The advantage of this Approach is that it takes a shared narrative, a story, and from this encourages children to devise questions that the whole class can discuss together in a **Community of Enquiry**. Some of the teachers found Robert Fisher's books helpful and each school bought a set for reference. They also bought sets of picture books to use as a stimulus for discussing questions together as advocated by Karin Murris in *Teaching Philosophy with Picture Books* (now revised and published as *Storywise* with Joanna Haynes).

> The **Community of Enquiry** Approach complements literacy hour teaching. It promotes questioning and discussion at (and beyond) text level.

The next step was to find space in the crowded primary curriculum. Originally, it was hoped that links could be made with humanities topics but this proved to be too artificial at times and so the stories and discussion became a supplement to the Approach advocated in the National Literacy Strategy or Literacy Hour.

One important development was that teachers made notes which recorded any modifications they made to the Approach and the reasons for making any changes. The teachers felt there were many points of contact between the structure *of Philosophy for Children* and the Literacy Hour, and the **Community of Enquiry** ensured that emphasis on speaking and listening was not lost. Wherever possible, the link with humanities was retained by choosing appropriate stories.

Setting up the Community of Enquiry

Although the teachers had little previous knowledge of thinking skills programmes, they were able to support each other as two teachers from each school were trialling the Approach and all the teachers met together to compare notes and share ideas. During the previous year, teachers in each school had been able to observe a demonstration of a **Community of Enquiry**, one in each Key Stage (5 - 7 years and 7 - 9 years), given by the University team as a pilot for the project. The Approach used in the schools was based on the following model, although individual teachers introduced their own adaptations. The teachers:

- identified stories that were thought provoking and likely to lead to further discussion;
- shared the story with the whole class (just as at story-time);
- gave the children enough time to think of interesting questions relating to the story: this was be done as a class, in groups, pairs or as individuals depending on the age of the children and their familiarity with the Approach;
- asked the children to prioritise questions so that there were no more than ten to discuss as a whole class.

The following points were also noted as important.

- Younger children require more help in selecting questions. It is helpful to manage the whole task as a class or use a supporting adult to facilitate groups by scribing questions.
- When choosing the questions for discussion it was more effective when this was done in pairs and then small groups. This way there was some peer review and discussion which usually weeded out unproductive questions.
- The whole class should come together to consider the ten (or so) chosen questions. Seating the children in a circle and displaying the selected questions promotes quality discussion.

> The **plenary** or **debriefing** phase of a teaching thinking lesson is crucial. It needs to focus not just on *what* has happened and *how* the lesson went but on evaluating *why* particular questions were valuable.

- The **Community of Enquiry** develops as each question is discussed, with children volunteering suggestions and counter-arguments. Any child may speak but all comments must be pre-fixed with, 'I agree with ... because...' or 'I disagree with ... because ...'.

- Only one child may speak at a time and all the children should be encouraged to listen carefully to responses.

- The children quickly assume the conventions of the **Community of Enquiry** and can become skilful at conducting their own discussions.

- The plenary session should focus on the types of question and discuss their relative merits. *Why was that a good question to discuss?*

- The plenary should also be used to give feedback and encouragement to pupils who listened well to others and built on what others have said.

Gathering the data

In order to make the project manageable, each school focused on one of the teachers and their class with another teacher following the model for the **Community of Enquiry** and keeping teachers' notes. During the Spring Term, both teachers in the school planned a minimum of 6 sessions during which they collected the pupils' questions. They made notes on the types and frequency of questions and the involvement of pupils in the discussions. In particular, the notes recorded any teacher led modifications to the Approach and the reasons.

At the end of the spring term, all the questions were collected in from the schools. The questions were analysed using a set of categories developed from the pilot for the project. We were interested in seeing whether there were any significant trends in the types of questions and whether there were any differences by age group or gender.

Previous research into the impact of a **Community of Enquiry** Approach on literacy carried out in one LEA in Wales (Dyfed, 1995) had demonstrated significant gains, particularly for younger children. Reading comprehension assessments were carried out at the beginning and end of the project in order to measure any potential impact to reading. The tests were not designed to measure specific aspects of the teaching such as, for example, the ability to respond critically to a text nor to focus on understanding of narrative texts only. The results were not conclusive, though improvement in two year groups (Y2 and Y4) on average exceeded what would have been expected during the length of the project.

Teachers' responses

The evaluations by the teachers at the end of the project were overwhelmingly positive. Everyone reported beneficial effects for the children in their classes. The value of the intervention for those participating lay in its impact on the patterns of classroom interaction, with pupils being more actively involved in the lessons and contributing to the discussions more effectively. All the teachers commented on the level of engagement and the extent to which pupils were willing and able to take responsibility for their own learning. A range of positive characteristics was identified.

'Children have:
- *improved their ability to question and justify choices;*
- *been able to participate regardless of ability;*
- *had opportunities to express themselves other than on paper;*
- *developed appropriate social skills and have worked well in teams;*
- *transferred skills to other areas'.*

Benefits for the whole class have had a particularly strong impact on individual pupils where the teacher has been able to identify strengths evident in the quality of questioning and discussion that had not been apparent in previous work.

Important findings

Community of Enquiry is a valuable Approach in teaching thinking. It offers the opportunity to develop a particular style of classroom interaction which teachers and pupils report that they enjoy. It supports the development of pupils' questioning skills and can enhance literacy teaching by promoting discussion at and beyond text level. However, the type of text selected is important. Fables and traditional stories often produce the best discussions. This may be because the stories are familiar enough to the children that they can focus on issues within the stories. Texts with unfamiliar settings produced a lot of questions at a purely factual level.

Possible development

The **Community of Enquiry** is a powerful teaching or pedagogical tool. Teachers we have worked with have used it to investigate and develop a range of classroom issues. These have included:

- increasing participation in whole class discussion;
- developing reasoning and interactive discussion;
- improving listening to others;
- involving isolated pupils;
- improving the quality of pupils' questions;
- improving turn-taking and respect for others' opinions.

> The choice of text is important. Traditional stories and fables often produced valuable questions which promoted discussion.

If you would like to investigate this for yourself then choose one of these objectives, collect some data before you start, then try out the Approach for a term. Towards the end of the term collect some further data and evaluate whether or not it has had an impact on that objective.

For example you might want to see if building a **Community of Enquiry** over the course of a term could help pupils listen and respond to each other's responses. To do this you could make notes during an early session to see how often pupils referred to what earlier contributors had said. This might include whether or not they used the conventions of 'I agree... because...' or 'I disagree... because...' and then some notes of words or phrases that indicated their contribution was building on an earlier one.

Have another go at collecting some data about half way through the term and think about whether the Approach is helping to achieve the goal you identified. An example of a straightforward data collection sheet is given below and in *Resource 1*.

> Try it out for yourself!
> 1. Identify an aspect of class discussion that you would like to improve.
> 2. Introduce the class to **Community of Enquiry** and use it once a week or so over a term.
> 3. Collect some data as you begin...
> 4. Again at the middle of the term...
> 5. And at the end of the term...
> 6. Analyse what you think has happened.

Name:	Agree/ Disagree/ Because	Notes
Sophie	(her question)	Reason: wolves eat pigs.
David	D, B	Not fair, pigs should live where they want.
Anita	A	(with David), wolves shouldn't have eaten them.
Michael	D, B	(with Anita), wolves eat meat, not vegetarian.

Ideally, it is helpful to work with a colleague who is also interested in investigating the Approach in their own classroom. You may even get some support from your headteacher to watch each other or take notes for each other; it can be hard to manage this on your own.

The idea is to use the Approach as a support to develop and extend the range of techniques you can use in the classroom. In our experience, developing **Community of Enquiry** as an Approach can improve the quality of classroom discussions, the quality of pupils' questioning, and their skills in listening and reasoning. We are not suggesting that you try to 'prove' scientifically that the Approach is the cause of the change. Classrooms are such complex places that the reasons for the success (or failure) of many innovations are more to do with the beliefs and enthusiasms of teachers than any guarantee that a particular approach will ensure a particular outcome. However, many teachers have found that the structure of a **Community of Enquiry** develops professional expertise and improves the quality of class discussion and reasoning.

Resource 1   Date:

Investigating the Community of Enquiry

Book/Text..

Name:	Agree/ Disagree/ Because	Notes

Suggestions for further reading

Dyfed
Improving Reading Standards in Primary Schools (1995, Dyfed LEA)

Fisher R.
Stories for Thinking (1996, Nash Pollock ISBN: 189825509)
See pages 14-15 in particular for advice on getting started.

Fisher R.
(Teaching Thinking: Philosophical Enquiry in the Classroom (1998, Cassell ISBN: 030470065)

Lipman
Philosophy goes to School (1998, Temple University Press)

Murris K.
Teaching Philosophy with Picture Books (1992, Infonet)

(NB This book is out of print but has been extensively revised and re-published by Karin Murris and Joanna Haynes as Storywise: Thinking Through Stories *(2001, Dialogue Works: Newport ISBN 1903804000). For further information, see the Dialogue Works website at:* **www.dialogueworks.co.uk**

Rosenshine B., Meister C. & Chapman S.
'Teaching pupils to generate questions: a review of intervention studies' in *Review of Educational Research 66,2* pp181-221(1996)

Splitter L.J. & Sharp A.M.
Teaching for Better Thinking – The Classroom Community of Inquiry (1995, ACER)

Sources of information on the World Wide Web

Although it is almost impossible to keep references to sources of information on the internet up to date, there is considerable information available, partly because the WWW offers such potential for the development of electronic or virtual communities of enquiry. As a result there is a thriving *Philosophy for Children (P4C)* presence on the Internet. The home of *P4C* is at the *Institute For The Advancement of Philosophy For Children* at Montclair State University. The founder of *P4C*, Matthew Lipman's site also has links to the Institute for Critical Thinking and other links of interest. It can be found at: **http://chss.montclair.edu/iapc/homepage.html**

In the UK, philosophy for children is promoted by SAPERE (the Society for the Advancement of Philosophical Enquiry and Reflection in Education) whose web site is at: **http://www.sapere.net**

The Society offers information and training about the Approach. If these links become outdated a search engine is likely to provide links quickly to the organisations involved or to the Approach.

9
Developing mental calculation strategies through metacognition

'But you think all you need to do to learn accounts is to come to
me and do sums for an hour or so, two or three times a-week;
and no sooner do you get your caps on and turn out of doors
again, than you sweep the whole thing clean out of your mind...
You think knowledge is to be got cheap - you'll come and pay
Bartle Massey sixpence a week, and he'll make you clever at
figures without your taking any trouble. But knowledge isn't to
be got with paying sixpence, let me tell you: if you're to know
figures, you must turn 'em over in your own heads, and keep
your thoughts fixed on 'em...'

George Eliot *Adam Bede (1859)*

9 Developing mental calculation strategies through metacognition

Rationale

Mental calculation is central to the development of effective calculating skills and underpins an effective understanding of our number system. The emphasis on improving both the competence and the confidence of pupils to calculate mentally is the lynchpin of the National Numeracy Strategy's *Framework for Teaching Mathematics* used in England. Yet there is no agreed vocabulary to describe the strategies that children of primary age typically use themselves, nor a complete progression of mental strategies set out in the *Framework* itself. If these strategies need to be taught to pupils then both teachers and pupils require a language to describe the mathematical processes being learned. For example most teachers and pupils talk about 'doubling' as a mental strategy, typically used by young children as they learn to work confidently with numbers to 20; perhaps related to their familiarity with dice games and dominoes. A related strategy would then be using the knowledge that double 8 is 16 to recognise that $17 = 8 + 8 + 1$ or $15 = 8 + 8 - 1$ which can then be called a 'near doubles' strategy. Arguably a more crucial strategy is knowing and being able to use numbers which add up to 10 or 'complements in 10'. It is more important because being able to calculate to and through multiples of 10 and then 100 uses the structure of our counting system. It leads to the strategy of 'partitioning' and 'bridging through 10' in double-digit addition and subtraction. However, there is not a commonly used term to describe this method when working with pupils. In the Netherlands, the Realistic Mathematics Project uses pictures of paired hearts to teach which two numbers add up to 10. This is then built upon later when teaching that a 'complements in 10' strategy is useful by showing two 'love-hearts' as icons at the top of an activity sheet. It is important to develop a vocabulary to describe the process of learning within a subject like mathematics as well as about learning more broadly. Both of these aspects of **metacognition** are important in effective teaching and learning.

> The focus of this chapter is developing an effective vocabulary in mathematics to describe strategies for mental calculation.

Developing pupils' articulation of mental strategies provided the focus for two related approaches. The first was using games to provide a context for teaching mental strategies. The second was adopted by a group of four first schools where the teachers extended the oral/mental starter of daily mathematics lessons by five minutes to allow sufficient time for discussion of mental strategies.

Procedure

> Using terms for strategies, such as 'near doubles' or 'bridging through 10' develops a vocabulary of strategies in mental calculation, and supports metacognition in mathematics.

1. Demonstrate a strategy (or elicit it from the pupils).

2. Model use of the strategy.

3. Provide time for pupils to practise and for you to assess informally.

4. Debrief key points during learning.

5. Review the strategy (using an appropriate term to describe it).

6. Identify where it can be used or how it can be applied more broadly.

The review process can be summarised as follows:

- What did you do?
- How did you do it?
- Why was that effective?

Games and Names

A small group of teachers in the North East used a range of number games designed to support the development of particular mental strategies. These teachers then planned to bridge the learning to other maths contexts, either through mental or practical activities with some explicit debriefing. The teachers worked in a range of classes from Year 1 to Year 5 and used a range of games once or twice a week as part of their maths lessons.

> Games are a great starting point for learning. But the learning often needs to be 'debriefed' before pupils can develop their understanding of what has been learned.

Whole class work

Following the structure of lessons advocated in the *Framework for Teaching Mathematics*, each of the games was introduced in the first section of the lesson. Sometimes this was with purely mental work using a strategy such as doubling to introduce *Double Cross Out (Resource 1)*, or by playing a giant version of the game with the class for *Zig-Zag Squares (Resource 4)*.

Main part of the lesson/group work

The games were then played in the main part of the lesson. Usually this was in pairs with the children sitting in larger organisational groups around tables of six or eight. This was most often the case where the activity was supported by another adult, or where different groups used slightly different versions of the games. On some occasions the games were used as independent activities (once the children were familiar with the rules and procedures) so that the teacher could focus on a particular teaching point with another group of children. Usually, however, the game formed a section of the lesson following the oral/mental introduction. Most of the teachers thought that this was most effective when some kind of review or debriefing was built into this part of the lesson, rather than being left until the plenary. This might include stopping the activity and having all of the pupils focus on the teacher or a pupil who could demonstrate a particular point. One example of this was in *Four in a Row (Resource 2)*, where the teacher asked one pupil to explain what was effectively a 'complements in 10' strategy to the class. This involved choosing two numbers that totalled 10 then adding a third number to reach the required total (ie if the target number is 17, then $6 + 4 = 10$, and $7 + 10 = 17$; or $8 + 2 = 10$, and 7 more takes you to 17) and asked the rest of the class to use this strategy for the remainder of the game. The teacher was able to remind them of the 'love-hearts' activity they had done earlier in the year where they had identified the 'partner' for each number to make 10. Similarly in *Race to 30 (Resource 5)*, one of the children realised that 23 is a crucial number to try to land on as you are then in a winning position. The teacher stopped the class and explained this with the child who had discovered the strategy, then asked the rest of the children to try it out. This technique of stopping and teaching a particular point seemed to help keep the pupils on track or focus their attention on the salient aspects of the activity. The pupils then had time to practise the strategy or skill during the lesson.

Plenary

The teachers all reported that as a result of trying to debrief the learning effectively and draw out important points of the lesson as they happened, they now found plenaries far harder than before! They realised it was not just a question of reviewing what had happened or even what had been learned in the lesson but that they were faced with some complex questions as the lesson developed:

- what needs to be consolidated or reinforced?
- what needs to be reviewed?
- how much of the review needs to focus on the process of learning (such as supporting the development of effective collaborative skills)?
- how much of the review needs to focus on the mathematical content?
- what connections can be made (within mathematics)?
- what learning can be 'bridged' to other contexts?
- is there anything about learning to learn that can be developed?

> Teaching thinking increases challenge. It not only challenges pupils, but challenges teachers.

Some of this can be planned in advance and likely points for **connections** or **bridging** can be identified, however effective review depends on the actual lesson and depends upon building positively and effectively on what the pupils have done. It is easy to go through the motions of reviewing the lesson and for it to have little or no impact on the pupils' thinking. This is particularly the case in a primary or first school as the children are either looking forward to play-time or lunch!

> It is not possible to cover all the potential teaching intentions in three achievable objectives.

Developing the Approach

Five examples of the games that the teachers used are included in the pages that follow. Some of these have been adapted for different age groups or to provide a sequence of lessons.

Double Cross Out has been used with a range of age groups and adapted as follows:

Year 1:   0-5, 1-6 dice;

Year 2:   5-10 dice, Multiples of 10 dice;

Year 3:   multiples of 100 dice; minutes and seconds dice;

Year 4:   halves and quarters dice; tenths decimals dice;

Year 5:   thirds dice ($^1/_3$, $^2/_3$, $1^1/_3$, $1^2/_3$, $2^1/_3$, $2^2/_3$); hundredths decimals dice (0.55 etc);

Year 6:   fraction dice; mixed decimals (0.6, 1.72, etc).

Some of the other games can be adapted similarly. A range of grids for *Four in a Row* can be developed using multiplication facts for example, or the game can be simplified by making three in a row the target for winning.

Make 10 (Resource 3) and *Zig-Zag Squares (Resource 4)* are not so flexible. They are both designed to support specific skills and a specific strategy. *Make 10* is designed to support and develop using complements in 10. It can be developed by changing the rules to use all of the numbers and making the winner the person who gets the most tens, or by changing the total and numbers to use. *Zig-Zag Squares* supports the skill of adding tens. It can also support the teaching of visual strategies in number using a 100 square, and links can be made with mathematical software, such as *Monty*. Different squares can be used (such as a vertically numbered 100 square or a square numbered from 201 to 300), though such variations should be tried with caution as part of the aim of the game is to help pupils see that adding 10 is the same as moving down one row. You can also use a blank 100 square as this will help develop the key idea. However, if the pupils have used different kinds of 100 squares you will need to write in at least 2 of the numbers. *Zig-Zag Squares* is based on a game used by Ian Sugarman (see his 'Teaching *for* Strategies' in Ian Thompson's *Teaching and Learning Early Number*, 1997, pp 142-154). The game is designed to teach children about the patterns in various regularly ordered 100 squares. The version here uses a square numbered from 1 to 100 so that the numbering of the square also represents the quantity involved. If you use a square with a zero you need to be aware that the square labelled 10 is actually the 11th square and this can be a cause of confusion for some children!

Race to 30 can be extended to 50, or even up to 100 with a choice of numbers up to 9. It will not work with dice as a key element is that players choose the numbers they want to use. The pupils have to think ahead and identify the key numbers to try to land on. Normally this starts with identifying the highest key number which is the final target number minus one more than the largest number you can play. So in *Race to 30* with the numbers 1-6 playable it is 23 that you aim for. If you play *Race to 100* with the numbers 1-9, then 90 is the key number. Of course, this gets more complex when you limit the number of choices as some numbers get used up in play. This can then form part of a deliberate ploy to outwit your opponent.

At the risk of causing confusion in the use of the word 'strategy' in this chapter there is a distinction between developing **mental strategies**, such as doubling or near doubles with games like *Double Cross Out* or *Four in a Row* or complements in 10 with *Make 10*, and developing **strategic thinking** with a game like *Race to 30* or in the positioning of your counters in *Four in a Row*. Both benefit from articulation, discussion, and explicit naming through metacognition. Of course, both of these are distinct, in turn, from the teaching thinking Strategies around which the *Section 1* of the book is written!

Double Cross Out

Resource 1

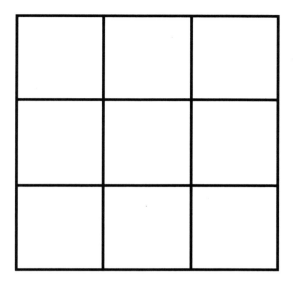

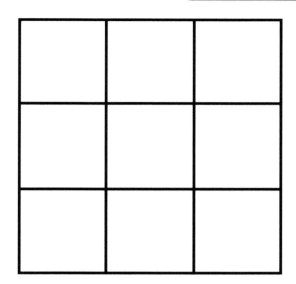

....'s grid   ....'s grid

You need:

A pencil each and one dice to share.

What you do:

Decide who goes first.

Take it in turns to roll the dice.

Double the number you rolled.

Write it in any box on your grid.

Carry on taking turns until your grid is full.

Now take it in turns to roll the dice again.

Double the number you throw.

If you have that number on your grid, cross it out.

To win:

The winner is the first person to cross out all their numbers.

Resource 2   Four in a Row

A game for two players

19	20	14	12	21	13	16
17	19	11	15	18	10	17
18	21	22	13	16	24	14
15	12	15	19	15	9	20
18	22	17	11	14	19	23
14	22	16	19	9	16	13
10	23	21	12	15	24	11

You need:
Two colours of cubes or counters and some scrap paper and pencils.

What to do:
Decide who goes first. Take it in turns to choose out loud any three of the numbers below. Add them up to make a number on the grid and cover that number with one of your colour of cubes or counters. You may double one number and add another. You must say out loud the numbers you are choosing such as "7 plus 5 plus 2 equals 14" or "double 5 plus 1 equals 11". Record the numbers you used on your scrap paper.

To win:
The winner is the first person to get four of their colour of cubes or counters in a row.

1 2 3 4 5 6 7 8 9

Make 10

Names...   ....

Player 1		Player 2	
1	1	1	1
2	2	2	2
3	3	3	3
4	4	4	4

You need:

A pencil each and a copy of this sheet.

What you do:

Decide who goes first. Take turns.

When it is your turn, choose a number from 1 - 4 and write it in a space in the grid. Cross it off your list. You have two of each number up to 4 to use. Cross out your numbers as you use them.

Keep playing until one row or column has 4 numbers in it that add up to 10.

To win:

You win if you are the first person to write in the number that makes a row or column add up to 10.

Resource 4   Zig-Zag Squares

You need:
A dice numbered 1,1,1,10,10,10 and a printed or blank 100 square for each player and two different coloured pencils.

What you do:
Decide who goes first. Take it in turns to throw the dice and count on the number you have scored (either 1 or 10). Colour that square in. (Write in the number if your square is blank.)

To win:
The winner is the person whose number 'trail' ends nearest to 100.

1	2	3	4	5	6	7	8	9	10
11	12	13	14	15	16	17	18	19	20
21	22	23	24	25	26	27	28	29	30
31	32	33	34	35	36	37	38	39	40
41	42	43	44	45	46	47	48	49	50
51	52	53	54	55	56	57	58	59	60
61	62	63	64	65	66	67	68	69	70
71	72	73	74	75	76	77	78	79	80
81	82	83	84	85	86	87	88	89	90
91	92	93	94	95	96	97	98	99	100

Race to 30

1	2	3	4	5	6	7	8	9	10	11	12	13	14	15	16	17	18	19	20	21	22	23	24	25	26	27	28	29	30

```
1  2  3  4  5  6
1  2  3  4  5  6
1  2  3  4  5  6
1  2  3  4  5  6
```

You need:

A copy of this game sheet and a pencil or pen for each player or pair of players.

What you do:

Decide who goes first. Take turns. The first player (or team) chooses a number from the box, crosses it out, then marks the jump on the number track and writes down the total. Then the next player (or team) chooses a number from the box, crosses it out and adds it to the total on the number track by drawing in the jump and making the total.

To win:

The winner is the first person (or team) to reach 30 exactly.

Exemplar 2

Sum Strategies

The pupils described and practised a range of mental strategies in mathematics. This is an example of metacognitive language.

The same four first schools in Northumberland that had been involved in investigating the **Community of Enquiry** and pupils' questioning discussed in *Chapter 8* decided to focus on improving children's mental calculation the following academic year. The focus chosen was partly due to the implementation of the *Framework for Teaching Mathematics* and partly to build on the speaking and listening skills developed the previous year. The aim of the project was to raise pupils' attainment in mental calculation in mathematics through developing their ability to articulate and describe the strategies that they used.

The project was funded from a range of sources including a Teacher Training Agency (TTA) Research Grant, in kind and actual funding from a local Single Regeneration Budget (SRB) project and the schools' in-service spending budgets.

In three lessons each week the teachers extended the length of the oral/mental starter of their mathematics lessons by five minutes. The additional time was used to provide more time for pupils to articulate and discuss the strategy or strategies that they used to solve a mental calculation. For example, when asked to calculate $23 + 23$, a range of strategies was proposed by pupils in one class:

'I know the answer . . .

double 23 is 46;

$20 + 20 = 40, 3 + 3 = 6, 40 + 6$ makes 46;

$23 + 20 = 43$, add 3 makes 46.'

The pupils were encouraged to share ideas and to evaluate the effectiveness of the different strategies that they used. The teachers explicitly taught and modelled strategies and vocabulary from the National Numeracy *Framework*. Teachers also helped pupils' learning by reinforcing different or more efficient strategies that were articulated and described or by modelling and showing ways to overcome particular difficulties that they encountered.

Collecting and recording assessments

The teachers' assessment of pupils' strategies was central to the project.

The discussions in the oral/mental part of the lesson often provided information about the pupils' learning which could be used in future teaching. The teachers therefore decided to collect information more systematically for a period of time. The schools identified sufficient money for each of the teachers to have a lesson of classroom support each half term to record the strategies that pupils were using.

They carried out individual interviews with some of the pupils in order to record how they explained their mental calculation strategies (*Resource 6*). The questions were based on examples of calculations for each year group in the National Numeracy Strategy *Framework*. The explanations were recorded on these formative assessment sheets, which were retained and discussed by teachers at professional development meetings involving teachers from all of the schools. The assessment sheets *(Resource 6)* were based on an activity from the NNS *Guide for your Professional Development Book 4*.

These half-termly support meetings also provided a forum for teachers to discuss issues related to teaching and learning. Input from staff in the Education Department at the University of Newcastle focused on the advantages and disadvantages of different teaching methods, progression in mental calculation in the numeracy framework, teaching thinking and pupils' learning, as well as practical activities and the use of a range of resources for teaching mathematics.

Gathering the data

One major benefit of the project was that teachers spent some time with individual pupils discussing mental calculation strategies and recording the pupils' responses. Part of this data collection was made possible by providing each teacher with half a day of classroom support each half term so that they could interview the pupils more systematically. All of the pupils were able to describe to some extent how they had carried out a calculation, even in Reception classes.

An example of a discussion between a Reception pupil and teacher:

Teacher: What comes before 6 when you are counting?

Pupil: 5, I counted backwards from 6.

Teacher: How do you know?

Pupil: Dad showed me how.

(Strategy: *counting back*)

An example of a discussion between a Year 2 pupil and teacher:

Teacher: 6 + 5?

Pupil: 11

     5 + 5 + 1 more.

(Strategy: *using near doubles*)

An example of a discussion between a Year 4 pupil and teacher:

Teacher: 560 + 575?

Pupil: Double 500 is 1,000

     Split 75 into 40 + 35

     Add 60 and 40, is 100.

     Then add 35 is 135.

     1,000 and 135 is 1,135.

(Strategy: *doubles, partitioning, complements*)

The close focus on pupils' responses was an important part of the development work in that it highlighted the range of strategies that were and were not being used by pupils. It therefore gave the teachers an opportunity to extend the use of different strategies in subsequent lessons.

The above examples show that pupils were generally able to articulate the strategies they used. Quite often they were able to provide a name or descriptive word for the strategy they used. In articulating their strategies, pupils were developing their **metacognitive** skills, helping them to be aware of and learn about and their own thinking and learning. When they used terms to describe strategies, rather than just describing how they manipulated the numbers they were credited with using **metacognitive** language.

Surprisingly the younger pupils (in Reception and Year 1) showed the greatest frequency of using **metacognitive** language in this way, often indicating that they had 'counted on', 'counted back' or 'counted in tens'. Older pupils reported that they had 'used doubles' or 'split' two and three digit numbers.

The greater use of metacognitive language for strategies by younger pupils may well reflect the level of modelling and guidance given to them by the teacher, including the use of appropriate language for the strategy, so developing explicitly shared meanings in the learning process.

Providing words and a language for learning helps the articulation of thought.

Teachers of older children may assume a greater shared understanding and spend less time making things explicit. The identification of strategies and terminology within the National Numeracy Strategy *Framework* gives the basis for a shared vocabulary, though the terminology for strategies is at times rather general, such as with 'compensation' and 'partition and recombine'. It may also be the case that the teachers involved were less familiar with the terminology for the two-digit strategies. This finding certainly suggests that there may be a need for teachers of older children to spend more time modelling strategies and identifying an appropriate vocabulary to describe them. It may also indicate that many pupils find using mathematical vocabulary challenging and need time and discussion to reinforce their understanding.

The teachers involved in the project reported that pupils' confidence was higher and attributed this to spending more time on the oral/mental part of the lesson. This was confirmed by an OFSTED inspection undertaken in one of the schools towards the end of the project where the pupils' confidence and competence at mental calculation was positively reported. The pupils' confidence may also have been higher as a result of learning that they could learn strategies and get better at mental calculation rather than it just being something that they were 'good at' (or not). Pupils who believe that their ability is not fixed respond more positively to challenge because they see it as an opportunity to learn.

Teachers' views

The teachers involved in the project reported greater confidence in their teaching of mental calculation. They indicated three factors contributing to this:

- the suggestions for practical activities opened up a pathway for progression in mental calculation and made taking action easier;
- the interviews with pupils provided insight into pupils' strategies and mathematical thinking;
- their knowledge and understanding of mental strategies and understanding of progression in this aspect of mathematics developed.

> The interviews with pupils were an example of diagnostic assessment which helped inform subsequent teaching.

The teachers indicated that they valued having test results and information from interviews with their pupils. This data helped them both to plan lessons and activities and to target their attention and questioning. The information helped identify secure knowledge as well as misconceptions. The opportunity to undertake the mental strategy assessments with classroom support was particularly welcomed though useful information was also gathered in more general terms at class or group level in the oral/mental part of the mathematics lesson. The extra time allowed for discussion of strategies in the first part of the mathematics lesson assisted with this process. As teachers became more familiar with the progression and strategies and the expectations for pupils in the NNS *Framework*, assessment information could be used to identify next steps for learning.

Some findings

- The articulation of strategies and the use of appropriate mathematical vocabulary helped the pupils to be aware of their learning and to become better learners.
- Teachers' modelling of mental calculation strategies was important in increasing their pupils' understanding.

> 'Debriefing' is crucial. It needs to focus not just on *what* has been done but on *how* as well as *why* a particular strategy was effective.

- Pupils were generally able to articulate the strategy they were using, although on occasions more precise vocabulary would have helped them explain how they had worked out particular calculations.
- Extending the oral/mental starter to the mathematics lesson produced benefits in the pupils' learning because it gave pupils the opportunity to articulate and discuss their strategies.
- Standardised mathematics tests showed significant improvement in pupils' performance (though it is not possible to attribute this to the project as the schools were involved in implementing the *Framework for Teaching Mathematics*).

Possible development

Articulation and discussion is essential in mathematics to develop understanding. It is essential at two levels. The pupils need to be able to describe what they are doing to avoid learning purely procedural skills based on an algorithm they will forget. The teacher also benefits from this articulation and discussion by identifying skills and understanding that is secure, and areas of uncertainty or misconception which need to be addressed.

If you would like to investigate this for yourself then first undertake an assessment of the mental strategies that your pupils are using, then focus on one or two strategies that you would like the pupils to use over the course of a half term. At the end of the half term undertake another assessment and evaluate whether or not it has had an impact.

To develop the strategies you could use or adapt some of the games from the previous exemplar. Most pupils will need plenty of examples to practise on. Try to develop pupils' use of an appropriate name for the strategy you want them to use such as:

- *near doubles* for calculations involving adding or subtracting one or two to a double that they know;
- *partners* for complements in ten (or 100);
- *over jump and step back* for adding 9s or 19s by adding 10 or 20 and subtracting 1 (can be modelled effectively on a number line);
- *leap and hop* for adding 11 or two digit numbers such as 32 or 21 by adding the tens first and then the ones (can be modelled effectively on a number line);
- *split and stick* for partitioning and recombining numbers (can be modelled with a diamond diagram).

Have another go at collecting some data towards the end of the half term and evaluate whether the approach has helped to achieve the goal you identified. An example of a completed assessment sheet adapted from the National Numeracy Strategy training materials is given below. A blank version for photocopying is included as *Resource 6*.

As with the previous chapter, it is helpful to work with a colleague or colleagues who are also interested in developing mental strategies in their own classrooms. You may even get some support from your headteacher so that you can work with the class while your colleague undertakes the pupil interviews.

> **Plan for teaching mental strategies:**
>
> 1. assess what strategies pupils are using;
>
> 2. introduce and name a strategy (or elicit one from a pupil);
>
> 3. model the strategy (or ask a pupil to);
>
> 4. adapt or design an activity to support it;
>
> 5. debrief during the activity;
>
> 6. review the strategy;
>
> 7. assess what strategies pupils are using.

Mental calculation: teacher notes sheet

Objective	Question	Comments
Identify near doubles, using doubles already known.	8+7 10+11	14, in head. 8+8=16, and I took 1 away 15. 21. 10+10+1 more.
Add/subtract 9 or 11, Add/subtract 10 and adjust by 1.	16+9 13+11 17−9	Count 4 then it's 20, then 5 more=25 (partitions and bridges). 24. I counted 11 from 13 (10 fingers + wrist). 7. What does 8+8 make? It's confusing (child giggles).
Use patterns of similar calculations.	If 17−9=8 and 27−9=18 and 37−9+28, what is 47−9?	17, (counts back in ones). That would be 8. 38.
State the subtraction corresponding to a given addition.	If you know that 12+5=17, what two subtraction facts do you know?	None.
Bridge through 10 or 20, then adjust.	8+4 18+5	Child: 13, (counts on fingers). Whose turn is it next? 23, (child beams!).

Progress since last assessment
Doubles - recall accuracy improved

Next targets for teaching
Consolidate symbols + and −, subtraction facts − corresponding to addition. Concentration!! She stops using bridging method halfway through.

Resource 6 · Pupil's Name..

Class...Date.........................

Mental calculation: teacher notes sheet

....

Objective	Question	Comments

Progress since last assessment
Next targets for teaching

Summary

Mental calculation is central to developing an understanding of our number system and in being confident to use numbers effectively in school and out. Pupils can be taught mental strategies through games and other activities. However, they also need practice in talking about and describing these strategies as well as in applying them; this helps to develop confidence and success in their use. This articulation also has the advantage for the teacher in exposing their pupils' thinking for assessment. Teachers can use this feedback to intervene and develop understanding.

Where this approach has been used pupils have made measurable gains in standardised tests of mathematical attainment and OFSTED inspectors have been impressed with the approach praising the teaching in oral/mental mathematics and commenting postivitely on the speed, agility and enthusiasm demonstrated by the pupils.

Suggestions for further reading

Mike Askew draws out some of the complexity of just what it means to be an effective teacher in 'It ain't (just) what you do: effective teachers of numeracy' in *Issues in Teaching Numeracy in Primary School* (1999, Open University Press).

The research literature suggests very strongly that pupils need to understand the causes of any errors or mistakes that they make. Paul Black & Dylan Wiliam have published extensively in this area: a succinct account is presented in *Inside the Black Box: Raising Standards through Classroom Assessment* (1998, Kings College). The team at Kings College argue persuasively that children should not be given feedback about their work in the form of the number of their correct answers (such as marks out of ten) but instead be given information about the sort of mistakes that they have made. This kind of formative assessment is helpful because it makes the purposes of tasks more explicit in a way that the learner can understand. It also encourages them to see that they can take some responsibility for improvement themselves.

Ian Sugarman's chapter 'Teaching *for* Strategies' in I. Thompson *Teaching and Learning Early Number* (1997, Open University Press) is the basis for *Zig-Zag Squares* as well as an excellent source for thinking about how to teach strategies.

Ian Thompson's article in *Mathematics in School 28,5* describes a range of strategies that children use (available on the web from the Mathematical Association at: **http://www.m-a.org.uk/eb/mis/ms028e.htm).** Although there is no agreed terminology to describe these strategies, understanding how children approach calculations can be a good starting point for working with them in the classroom.

Some of the ideas for the maths games were developed in a series of articles by Steve Higgins & Rod Bramald in *Child Education* (Scholastic) called 'Numeracy Basics'. These were 'Adding to Ten' in *Child Education* (October 2000, pp 43-45); 'Adding 3 Numbers' in *Child Education* (November 2000, pp 41-43); and 'Place Value' in *Child Education* (December 2000, pp 37-39).

10
Using ICT to support thinking and reasoning

'*Each problem that I solved became a rule which served afterwards to solve other problems*'

Descartes *Discours de la Méthode (1637)*

10 Using ICT to support thinking and reasoning

Rationale

ICT offers a range of ways to support teaching thinking. At one extreme this could be just supporting teaching through the preparation of materials for lessons: either printed materials; or multimedia presentations where the pupils do not use the technology at all. At the other extreme it could involve pupils developing their ICT skills and using ICT to present and communicate their learning to a wider audience. *Chapter 14* looks at some of the ways that ICT can be mapped onto teaching thinking but the use of ICT in teaching thinking could be a book on its own!

Procedure

This chapter differs from the others in that there is no straightforward procedure to follow. The Exemplars are therefore more like case studies. They show how some teachers in the North East of England have used ICT to support teaching thinking. Both exemplify the principles of teaching thinking expounded in *Chapter 1*:

- clear purpose made explicit;
- articulation by the pupils;
- mediation by the teacher;
- connecting learning;
- evaluation by pupils;
- metacognition and discussion of learning.

The first case study is based on work undertaken in a Teacher Training Agency (TTA) funded research project on 'Effective Pedagogy using ICT for Literacy and Numeracy' in primary schools. Although the focus in that project was raising attainment through developing the use of ICT, the Approach followed by the teacher also illustrates the principles of teaching thinking.

> ICT is a complex tool. It can be used in a range of ways to support teaching thinking.

Multimedia Apostrophes

The teaching and learning issue

The teacher had used a number of different strategies to teach the correct use of apostrophes but found that more than half the class had not understood how to use them correctly especially when used for omissions or contractions. Given the amount of input which had taken place (for example, whole class teaching, individual worksheets, homework and even a demonstration using a feather duster to 'tickle out' letters!) the teacher was surprised and rather disappointed. She was therefore keen to try an Approach using ICT to make the rules of use explicit in order to improve the children's understanding and help them move from using *will'nt* to *won't*.

> ICT motivates pupils. This can be as a focus and purpose for creating a final product.

It was important to her to involve all the children in the use of ICT and not just those who were struggling with the correct usage. She wanted to make the problem explicit to the children in a way that they would understand and to make the purpose of the activities clear. In her planning for ICT capability she wanted to use a program which would also stretch their ICT skills and contribute to the teaching of ICT capability. Many of the children had computers at home and as a consequence some pupils had advanced ICT skills.

Screen from the 'Apostrophe Stack'

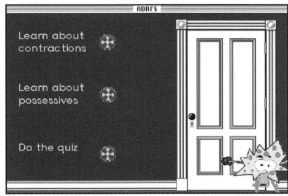

Existing ICT skills

The class had used a multimedia program previously to support a project on Ancient Greece. The work the children contributed to the project both at and away from the computer had been impressive. However, this program had proved difficult for some of the children to use and not all were able to take part in the computer activity because of the high level of ICT skills demanded by the program. A newer multimedia program renewed her enthusiasm because of its ease of use. The teacher was convinced that these pupils would rise to the challenge; especially a challenge where there would be a wider audience and purpose for their work.

The software

The teacher chose to use *HyperStudio* a multimedia program which allows pupils to mix text, graphics, sound and video so that the pupils could consider how to communicate their ideas effectively. As the teacher had never used this software before she was enthusiastic about learning alongside the pupils. The program assembles a series of pages or screens into a 'stack' or collection. You can design a route through the final presentation so that the user has choices and can go to different sections by clicking on 'buttons' on the page. Each page can have animations of pictures and words as well as sounds or even video. Considerable planning and thinking also goes into the design of a presentation, though this aspect of thinking skills is not the focus of this Exemplar.

Clear purpose

The children were told that they were going to produce a multimedia presentation which could be used by other children to help them understand the use of apostrophes. It was made clear to the children that although the final product would appear on the computer the majority of the work would take place away from the computer. This did not in any way dampen their enthusiasm.

The teacher hoped that the children could both enhance their ICT skills and improve their understanding of apostrophes by identifying how to teach aspects of correct usage to other children. In so doing they would develop their awareness and understanding of how to use apostrophes correctly themselves.

How the teacher developed the project

The teacher used a mind mapping and brainstorming session to get the project underway. The children were asked to come up with ideas on how they might teach the use of apostrophes to other pupils. Initially they could only come up with *'test them'*. Further discussion led by the teacher produced more useful ideas with the children agreeing that if they could establish some rules and examples this might work. Discussions also took place about presentation with the children deciding they wanted a 'character' who appeared when help was requested. Many other ideas were forthcoming, some discarded, others making their way into the final presentation.

A 'character' competition was organised where all the pupils submitted a drawing; the drawings were all displayed with pupils voting for their top three. This enabled the whole class to work on the project at the same time and increased the motivation for the task as well as supplying a deadline for completion. In additional sessions children worked on colour schemes, and planned the layout of the 'stack' (the series of multimedia pages which made up the presentation). They also agreed on what the rules might be for omissive apostrophes (eg *it's* and *didn't* but not *children's* which is an example of a possessive apostrophe) and came up with hints, tips and examples of use.

Articulating patterns and rules

The session with the children where they finally decided on the rules is worth particular consideration. It involved the children in word level work distinguishing different uses of apostrophes as well as sentence level work identifying patterns in how apostrophes were used. In pairs the children were given a list showing the original two words followed by the contraction eg *you are* ➡ *you're*. They were asked to use colour pencils to highlight groups which they thought were similar. Many children looked at the number of missing letters and created a grouping this way. Others came up with more sophisticated patterns. Once they had finished, a whole class discussion took place on what the groups had found and finally a consensus was reached which everyone agreed to and understood.

Screen showing some of the pupils' rules

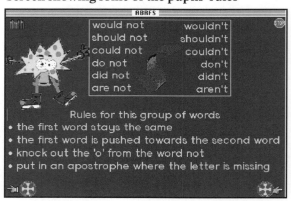

Making the rules explicit through mediation

The teacher thought that encouraging the children to formulate their own rules for apostrophe usage was a powerful teaching strategy:

> *'Asking the children, rather than telling them that 'this is the rule', 'it always does this', is more powerful. Asking them, in groups, to find the rules and report back in a plenary session is a good way to get them to focus upon a particular aspect.'*

She found that she could support the development of understanding through effective discussion and questioning both during the group and plenary stages of this process.

ICT as a catalyst for thinking

Only at this stage did work begin on the computer. The children had assistance with

The teacher 'launched' the work with a brain storming session. This provided an opportunity to get feedback about the pupils' thinking.

This is an example of an important skill: **classification**.

The teacher used the discussion to discuss categories and articulate rules about how omissive apostrophes are used.

assembling some aspects of the 'stack' or series of multimedia slides but were confident in adding pictures, sound, linking pages and creating simple animations. The completed multimedia stack was demonstrated to parents, governors and other members of staff who were suitably impressed with the pupils' understanding of creating multimedia presentations as well as their knowledge of apostrophes. The ICT had acted as a catalyst for the class. They worked enthusiastically together on what is potentially a rather dry subject.

The teacher used ICT as a vehicle to encourage the children to work as a team. Although the multimedia presentation was considered by the children as the final result, for the teacher it was the thinking that had gone into establishing the rules, agreeing the examples, hints and tips and working collectively as a class that was important. In moving their understanding of omissive apostrophes forward, the work that had taken place away from the computer was more important than what had actually been achieved using the computer.

Understanding through discussion

As the project unfolded the teacher became increasingly aware of how complex the teaching of this particular aspect of word and sentence level work was. The teacher was impressed with the quality of discussion which took place in the whole class sessions and with the effort the children put into trying to make meaning for other students. As with her project on Ancient Greece she felt it was the creation of multimedia and the preparation work which that entailed which had benefited the children's learning and not just the use of the technology. The teacher was not convinced that the use of the completed presentation would necessarily move other children's understanding of apostrophes forward, though the children could have used it to try it out on their peers.

Metacognition: learning through thinking

In this project the teacher was able to use ICT effectively to develop pupils' understanding of a challenging aspect of word level work. The work was planned around the computer. However, less work was undertaken by the pupils actually using computers than in whole class and group sessions where ICT was not used. Although this was in part due to the fact the class have only one computer permanently available, the teacher said she would choose to repeat the Approach to create a multimedia presentation in the same way because of the quality of work the children produced away from the computer in the whole class and group sessions.

As the work progressed she realised that the teaching of apostrophes was more complex than she had previously thought and that this perhaps explained some of the difficulties she had experienced in teaching this aspect of word level work before. Omissive apostrophes are complex. Some follow a pattern such as *didn't* and *wouldn't* but then other similar contractions, such as *won't*, do not. The approach she took enabled her to understand the difficulties the children were having and use this knowledge to improve their understanding.

The Approach also focused the children's attention on the rules and patterns of apostrophe use and encouraged them to make these rules explicit through observation and discussion. This metacognitive Approach encourages learners to articulate and make explicit what they are thinking about their own learning.

Further reading

The development work described in this Exemplar is based on research funded by the Teacher Training Agency (TTA). It is published in a series of 12 illustrations of developing effective practice using ICT in *Ways Forward with ICT: Effective Pedagogy using Information and Communications Technology in Literacy and Numeracy in Primary Schools*. The report about this project was written by a team led by David Moseley and Steve Higgins and published by the Education Department at the University of Newcastle upon Tyne in 1999. The report and illustrations are available on the web: **http://www.ncl.ac.uk/education/ttaict**.

Some helpful suggestions to tackle aspects of punctuation can be found in Waugh's 'Practical Approaches to Teaching Punctuation in the Primary School' (in *Reading 32, 2* pp14-17).

Troutner's article 'Yes, they put on quite a show but what did they learn?' (in *Technology Connection 3* pp 15-17) looks at the development of a framework to assess multimedia projects. Collins, Hammond & Wellington's *Teaching and Learning with Multimedia* (1997) describes a range of projects and approaches which could form the basis of thinking through ICT.

Exemplar 2

Meet the Zoombinis!

Teaching and learning aims

The Zoombinis Maths Journey (originally released as *The Logical Journey of the Zoombinis*) is a captivating critical thinking program designed around a journey of escape. The puzzles in the program require the use of logical and deductive reasoning and thinking. Each of the puzzles is different and has different levels making it suitable for a range of ages, though in our experience pupils aged 8 and older will benefit most from explicit teaching of Strategies based on the software.

The program

The Zoombinis are a colourful and happy race of creatures whose island is taken over by invading and exploiting creatures called Bloats. The player's job is to help them in their escape and create a new homeland. It is an unconventional mathematics program, in that numbers and arithmetical operations do not play much of an explicit role. Instead, this program focuses on the logic and reasoning elements of mathematics: attributes, matching, patterns, groupings, sorting, comparisons, and problem solving. There are links to mathematical and scientific reasoning, as well as with geography and history (are the Zoombinis invaders or settlers?), as well as the potential for developing collaborative skills in speaking and listening. The links with teaching thinking and developing logical reasoning are evident. The challenge for the teacher is to find a place in the overcrowded curriculum to spend sufficient time for pupils to benefit from using it.

The puzzles

Each Zoombini has one of five different types of hair, eyes, colour of their nose, and feet. It is therefore possible to have 625 different combinations of these features. Once you have chosen your group of 16 Zoombinis, you have to help them to overcome a dozen different obstacles using deductive logic and creative reasoning. For example, the first obstacle in their path is a pair of rope bridges at the Allergic Cliffs. One of the two guardians of these cliffs sneezes if a Zoombini with the wrong feature (or combination of features) tries to cross his bridge. If you make too many mistakes, the bridge collapses. This requires children to use evidence to work out how to get all of their group of Zoombinis across without the bridge collapsing.

Teaching for transfer

Because the pupils understand the purpose of the game they quickly become involved in the program. The disadvantage of this is that they do not automatically see the links with the mathematical logic that they are using. We have made two different links in teaching about this first puzzle with mathematical diagrams. A Venn diagram can be used to analyse the common features of the Zoombinis who have crossed the bridges. This is powerful because as each Zoombini is successful the two sets increase in size and it is possible to use the language of hypothesis and testing from science here to describe what is happening. One

Thinking Through Primary Teaching

teacher asked pupils *'What is your hypothesis?'* when supporting this puzzle. Or, in other words, *'What do you think is the distinguishing feature'* (or features at harder levels) *'that separates the two different groups or sets of Zoombinis who have successfully crossed the bridge?'* With a data projector or an interactive whiteboard the puzzle can be analysed with the class and this language reinforced. The disadvantage of this approach is that some children then think that both of the groups have some connecting feature. In fact, one group has a feature in common and the other group *lacks* that feature. One of the guardians is allergic to something and the other is allergic if they do not have it. So we have also tried using a decision tree structure to identify which bridge each Zoombini should cross. This involved asking the pupils to identify the question that they need to ask. For example *'Does this Zoombini have sunglasses?'* If yes then use the top bridge, if no then the bottom bridge. This enabled one teacher to ask pupils *'What do you think the question is?'* as he observed and supported pupils working on this puzzle.

> Understanding the logic of having a property or NOT having that property underpins classification as well as logical reasoning.

> Using a pupil's analogy or idea is powerful because it often communicates more effectively to the other children as well as valuing the original contributor.

Other activities include arranging the creatures on Captain Cajun's raft in a correct sequence where each Zoombini must have something in common with their neighbour. One pupil described this as *'like dominoes'*. The teacher was then able to use this description of the strategy to help other pupils to solve it. Other puzzles lend themselves to other mathematical diagrams. The puzzle at Stone Cold Caves is like a Carroll diagram. To get past the Fleens you can use a mapping diagram to show which attributes of the Zoombinis correspond to the attributes of the Fleens.

One of the most impressive features of this program is the potential it has for repeated use, across a broad range of ages. Each of the puzzles increases in complexity if you get all of your Zoombinis through. At the simplest level, five and six year olds have completed the puzzles through trial and error. The hardest levels of the hardest puzzles challenge adults! The disadvantage is that it is difficult to keep the class together and discuss strategies or solutions to particular puzzles. However the program also has a practice mode where the puzzles can be tried at four levels of difficulty. This can be useful for setting a specific challenge to teach particular skills and discuss successful strategies. One teacher used this Approach with a data projector in the ICT suite. Each session started by looking at a particular puzzle in practice mode. Each of the pairs and small groups tried it, then discussed their strategies as a class. The groups then returned to the game mode to continue their journeys.

Another class had used *'Top Ten Thinking Tactics'* by Mike Lake & Marjorie Needham and the teacher encouraged them to use the language of the tactics, such as 'Pinpointing the Problem' or 'Check and Change' to discuss and evaluate their progress.

The program has been used with different ages of pupils, from Year 3 to Year 6. It has been successfully managed in classrooms with a single computer as well as on a network where a whole class used it (in pairs) on a weekly basis. The summary of pupils' strategies below draws on its use in a number of these classrooms. In general, pupils collaborate well, though some need encouragement to share the mouse and to discuss and agree a course of action. The program quickly becomes challenging to even the most able who therefore found it useful to discuss what to do so that they did not lose any Zoombinis. Successful pairings varied, with higher attaining pupils sometimes being surprised at the ideas and suggestions of friends less successful at more traditional tasks. The level of motivation and task-related talk observed in all classes was high.

Pupils' strategies

At first most of the pupils that were observed using the program solved the puzzles by trial and error. A loose hierarchy of less to more successful approaches emerged:

- random attempts with no plan of action;
- randomly trying out a single idea (ie forgetting which Zoombinis they had used);
- systematic testing (working through the band of Zoombinis but with no clear hypothesis);
- systematic testing with a single idea;
- suggesting alternatives (some pupils found it difficult to change their minds);
- trying alternatives systematically (though it is easy to lose track);
- using feedback effectively (ie checking their idea was correct both for successful and unsuccessful attempts);
- developing a strategy for a type of problem, attacking it systematically and considering the implications of feedback to reach an effective solution.

> Identifying this progression in pupils' strategies is a type of diagnostic assessment.

Identifying this hierarchy helped some teachers to move their pupils on to becoming more systematic in their approach or paying more attention to the feedback they got from the program.

Articulation and discussion

The most successful pupils used a combination of approaches. In some of the puzzles you need to try something and risk making mistakes in order to get some feedback so that you can work out what to do, such as in *Di-dimensional Hotel*. In others, such as *Captain Cajun's Ferryboat*, you can plan a complete solution first and then move your Zoombinis. It certainly to helped to get pupils to explain how to solve the puzzles. Even some 'experts' found it difficult to articulate why they were being successful.

A specific set of help strategies evolved through discussion and debriefing with the class. This was for each pair of children working together to:

- talk about it with your with partner;
- agree what to do first;
- if you get stuck:
  - what is the problem?
  - what kind of puzzle is it?
  - what have you tried?
  - what idea are you going to try next?
  - how are you going to keep track of what you have done?

Then, if a pair felt that they needed further help, that they should:

- use a help sheet;
- ask a friend (is allowed to explain without touching the mouse!);
- ask an expert (who can suggest a strategy);
- ask the teacher (who may not be able to do it either!).

The addictive appeal of the game is such that it was hard to get pupils to use the help sheets and support materials we designed while they were on the computer. It was much more fun to play!

The Allergic Cliffs

Your first job is to guide the Zoombinis across the Allergic Cliffs. If one of the cliffs is allergic to one of a Zoombinis attributes, he'll sneeze you straight off the bridge. But if one cliff is allergic to a Zoombini, the other one won't be! You have just six chances to get them all across, so use the record sheets below to help you work out which feature each cliff is allergic to!

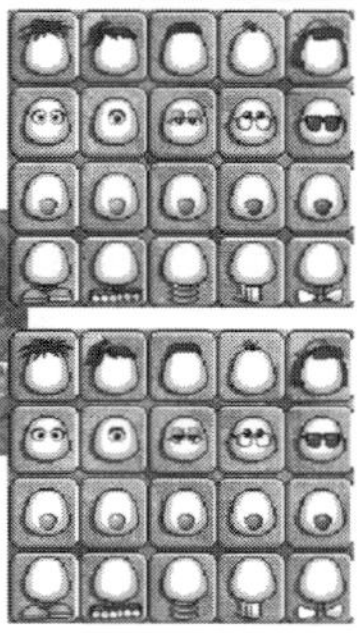

Use these attribute record cards to mark off which Zoombinis get across safely. It might help you work out what the cliff's allergy is to.

Don't forget to clean the card when you have finished!

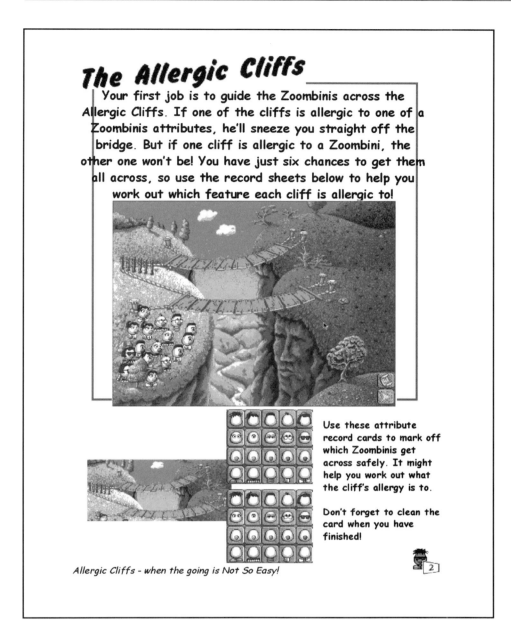

Allergic Cliffs - when the going is Not So Easy!

Mediation

As a teacher, knowing when to intervene directly is always difficult. Ideally, probing questions can support the pupils in structuring their ideas, but in practice this is hard to do. In the end it emerged that it was probably better to step in after a brief interval and explain how to solve the puzzle, then see if the pupils had understood the next time they faced a similar challenge. Of course, knowing the pupils was also essential, as some may request help too quickly. As the puzzles are always different they need to understand principles rather than solutions. Modelling or demonstrating a solution, or getting other pupils to demonstrate a strategy, while explaining *why* it works seemed to be the most helpful approach.

Modelling and explaining are important teaching skills.

Metacognition

Encouraging pupils to articulate their strategies was easiest with the whole class arrangement, as it was possible to begin and end sessions with a review or summary. Most children find it hard to grasp the idea that mistakes can help you learn. But as each puzzle offers four levels of challenge, and the difficulty level automatically increases as each full group of Zoombinis goes through, it is impossible not to make mistakes. Furthermore, the solutions are different with each attempt, so a player never faces exactly the same puzzle twice. The advantage of this is that pupils quickly see that you have to concentrate on principles and strategies. It is therefore possible to develop a shared language for discussing strategies for problem solving with the class.

Connecting learning

The pupils we observed and worked with certainly became more skilful at solving the problems in the program and more articulate in explaining their strategies and solutions. The crucial question is: does helping the Zoombinis on their journey mean that these children will think better in other situations? Is time spent with the Zoombinis going to have an effect in their English lessons or on their capacity to understand mathematics? This kind of **transfer** of learning from one situation to another is always difficult to show. From observations of the program being used by pupils and discussion with the teachers involved the most important factor is the role played by the teacher. Teachers can aid the **transfer** of skills by making the thinking strategies used with the Zoombinis more explicit and by drawing out connections with different areas. For example, the connection between problem solving in the Zoombini world with questioning and hypothesising in science can be developed. Specific puzzles can be solved with familiar mathematical diagrams. Used in this way the Zoombinis can help to develop logical thinking skills of the kind that are useful across the curriculum.

Summary

ICT is a tool that can be used by teachers and pupils to support teaching and learning. It is therefore a tool that also supports teaching thinking. It does not offer an easy solution: many of the teaching and learning problems are the same when using ICT as when using more traditional approaches. ICT can provide a lens to examine particular aspect of a teaching and learning situation and to alter the focus of the activity. The challenge is in using this to support the development of constructive thinking.

Further reading

An earlier account of this work investigating the use of this software by Steve Higgins & Nick Packard called 'Zoombini Power', appeared in the inaugural edition of *Teaching Thinking 1*, pp 12-14 (Questions Publishing Company).

Lyn Dawes, Neil Mercer and Rupert Wegerif's programme of talk lessons *Thinking Together* (2000, Questions Publishing Company) is based on research and designed to support effective talk and reasoning in small groups both at and away from the computer.

11
Effective teaching and teaching thinking

'It is not enough that certain materials and methods have proved effective with other individuals at other times. There must be a reason for thinking that they will function in generating an experience that has educative quality with particular individuals at a particular time.'

John Dewey *Experience and Education (1939)*

SECTION 3

11 Effective teaching and teaching thinking

Section 3 has two broad aims:

- to review and summarise the Strategies and Approaches covered in the earlier *Sections* of the book;
- to present an analysis of the research on effective teaching and how we believe this literature base connects with teaching thinking.

If this sounds dull, please keep reading! Rather like a plenary in a teaching thinking lesson we hope to review and extend the understanding of teaching thinking that was presented through the Exemplars. We have tried to build in review of the key ideas through the chapter summaries and the marginal notes as the book has progressed. However issues that were implicit in these short feedback loops in the earlier sections will benefit from a more explicit discussion of the underpinning principles of teaching thinking.

Review

Level 1 - Use the materials

Level 2 - Adapt and apply the Strategies

Level 3 - Debrief learning to develop metacognition

Level 4 - Infuse teaching thinking to develop more effective learning

In *Section 1* of the book the Exemplars show how particular teaching Strategies can support learning in the primary classroom. Most of these Strategies can be applied across the curriculum as single activities or more systematically to develop feedback and formative assessment making teaching more effective.

In *Section 2* of the book the Exemplars show how developing these Strategies and Approaches in teaching thinking can be infused or integrated as part of a programme of professional development.

These two *Sections* of the book covered the **Levels of use** discussed in the introduction:

Level 1: using or applying the teaching resources

Level 2: adaptation and development

Level 3: debriefing learning and metacognition

Level 4: infusion

The Strategies and Approaches

Odd One Out is designed as a quick whole class activity that supports conceptual thinking by pupils and informal assessment by the teacher, though it can be developed as a teaching strategy and a paired or collaborative task. **Living Graphs, Fortune Lines** and **Mysteries** are Strategies related by the way that they break text up into chunks and encourage pupils to make connections between the frame (the chart structure) or between the other pieces of information in a **Mystery**. These Strategies are designed to be introduced or 'launched' to the whole class but then worked upon collaboratively in small groups where this less formal collaborative discussion and articulation supports individual learning. Like **Odd One Out** these Strategies also encourage pupils to draw on their knowledge and experience from in school and out. **Writing frames** are scaffolding tools that can also be used to support explicit writing skills and discussion of genres of language. All of these Strategies benefit from **debriefing** the skills involved in the process of learning as well as the curriculum or subject content and can be used to foster positive attitudes to learning: they can develop a **vocabulary** *of* and *for* learning. These Strategies offered a key to open the door to the Approaches which followed.

The Exemplars for the Approaches show how the potential of teaching thinking can be further developed. **Community of Enquiry** supports pupils' enquiry and reasoning skills, more usually fostered in smaller groups, using a narrative or story structure to generate questions and interactive discussion at whole class level. The nature of classroom interaction changes, scaffolded by the formal structuring of the discussion. The Approaches to developing metacognition in mathematics identifies how teaching *for* strategies and explicit articulation and discussion of mathematical language as a discrete part of a focussed mathematics lesson can support pupils' learning and teachers' understanding. This process of making learning explicit is again picked up in the ICT Exemplars where teaching thinking is infused into the activities.

Effective teaching

There is an extensive and compelling literature on effective classroom teaching. Part of the recent research at Newcastle University has included a review of some of this published material. An earlier version of this analysis appeared as an appendix to an influential research report published by a team in the Education Department at Newcastle University on ICT and pedagogy (Moseley *et al*, 1999) and thanks must go to Frank Hardman, a member of that team, for the original summary and permission to develop it here. The review analyses some of the research on classroom interaction and summarises some of the findings and practical implications for teachers. The literature reviewed helps to set the Strategies and Approaches of teaching thinking and the method of professional development in a broader context. Its starting point is understanding different teaching or pedagogical approaches in order to match approaches with specific learning objectives and particular teaching and learning contexts. However, it must be borne in mind that learning objectives need to be considered within a specific time frame; and it is possible to criticise much of the school effectiveness research on either the basis of the measures of attainment and measures of effectiveness, or both! (Elliott, 1996). Educational goals may be short – achievable within a lesson or two; medium term – over a series of lessons or weeks; or long term – over the course of months or a year, or even longer. This applies in particular to the development of **metacognitive approaches**, and **teaching for transfer** which are exceedingly difficult (if not impossible) to achieve in the short term. Developing positive attitudes and a learning disposition can only be long term goals and preferably are part of a whole school approach.

The research on effective teachers and teaching indicates which approaches are *most likely* to be successful in a new context, particularly in the short term. However, any decision to use them must also evaluate to what extent the choice was successful in that new context and whether any alternatives offer the possibility of greater success, either in the short, medium or longer term. A focus on teaching thinking can act as a catalyst for professional development and allows many of the effective teaching behaviours outlined below to develop through the teachers' direct attention on pupils' learning and their developing understanding of particular curriculum tasks.

Knowing what to teach - subject principles

The King's College study of *Effective Teachers of Numeracy* (Askew, Brown *et al*, 1997) demonstrated that teachers' awareness of the connections and relationships within a subject contribute to their effectiveness. The model used in this study (above) maps out the relationship between teachers' underpinning beliefs in numeracy as well as their mathematical subject knowledge in an important way. One of their conclusions was that *'teachers' beliefs and understandings of the mathematical and pedagogical purposes behind particular classroom practices seemed to be more important than the forms of practice themselves'*. These beliefs and understandings must, however, be evident in teachers' actions in order to have an effect. That direct effect is hard to identify using the observational techniques in classrooms over a short period of time, and it is perhaps important to understand how a teacher's beliefs and intentions influences their actions, and in particular how these subtle differences add up over time.

Knowing how to teach content to pupils

Pupils start from different points in their experience and learning. There are, therefore, important social and psychological aspects of teaching and learning (see, for example, Wood (1998) for a summary). An effective teacher will seek to create the most effective conditions for learning for pupils from differing backgrounds and with different personal characteristics, competences and knowledge. Aubrey (1997) presents some implications of the knowledge of mathematics that different Reception pupils have on entry to school. The older pupils become, and the more diverse their experience and knowledge, the greater the challenge! Designing the teaching strategies which will be the most efficient or the most effective in balancing the needs of the majority as well as the particular or special needs of individuals is a real problem for all teachers. On the other hand schooling also leads to increased conformity by pupils that arguably reduces expectations and challenge in learning. Pollard (1985) describes this as a negotiated 'working consensus' and shows how pupils seek to close down open-ended tasks to reduce thinking and the risk of failure. Teaching thinking Approaches try to sustain diversity and individuality by encouraging pupils to draw on their own experience and knowledge in classroom tasks, and alter this consensus.

How teachers teach subject content is determined by their knowledge, understanding and experience of the process of teaching children. This is sometimes called pedagogical content knowledge following Schulman's work (1986). It involves knowledge and understanding of both content and children:

> Teaching thinking Strategies are a kind of pedagogical content knowledge.

> *'...the most regularly taught topics in one's subject area, the most useful forms of representation of those ideas, the most powerful analogies, illustrations, examples, explanations and demonstrations – in a word, the ways of representing and formulating the subject that make it comprehensible to others.... also include an understanding of what makes the learning of specific concepts easy or difficult: the conceptions and preconceptions that students of different ages and backgrounds bring with them to the learning.'*
>
> Schulman (1986)

> Teaching thinking gives teachers a practical starting point for action to change what happens in classrooms.

It is clear from research (such as *The Effective Teachers of Numeracy* study mentioned above) that these areas of knowledge are important in effective teaching: knowledge of content, or the subject being taught; knowledge about the way pupils learn; and then the combination of these - the way to teach *particular* content to *particular* pupils. Issues to do with organisation and the practicalities of managing teaching are important too, and this craft knowledge is what teachers use to make rapid decisions and is perhaps what helps teachers to be efficient. Brown & McIntyre (1993) show how teachers tend to evaluate their teaching in terms of what pupils do rather than evaluating their own behaviours, and tend to describe 'normal desirable states of pupil activity' related to relatively short term outcomes.

Research on effective teaching behaviours

From the research into classroom interaction, five effective teaching behaviours have been identified that researchers generally agree contribute to learning gain, regardless of context, at least as measured by classroom assessment and standardised tests in English and mathematics (Galton *et al*, 1980; Brophy & Good, 1986; Good & Brophy, 1991; Walberg,

1986; Croll & Moses, 1988; Mortimore *et al*, 1988; Brophy, 1986; Pollard *et al*, 1994). The effective teaching behaviours identified in the research are as follows:

1. **Lesson clarity;**

2. **Instructional variety;**

3. **Teacher task orientation;**

4. **Engagement in the learning process;**

5. **Pupil success rate.**

1. Lesson clarity

This key behaviour refers to how clear and interpretable a presentation is to the class. Research on clarity suggests teachers vary considerably on this behaviour: not all teachers are able to communicate clearly and directly to their pupils without wandering, speaking above pupils' levels of comprehension, or using speech patterns that impair the clarity of what is presented. Some indications of a lack of clarity (Brown & Wragg, 1993; Dillon, 1988) are:

- the extent to which a teacher uses vague, ambiguous, or indefinite language ('might probably be', 'tends to suggest', 'could possibly happen');

- the extent to which a teacher uses overly complicated sentences ('there are many important reasons for eating food but some are more important than others, so let's start with those that are thought to be important but really aren't');

- the extent to which a teacher gives directions that often result in pupil requests for clarification.

Teachers who teach with a high degree of clarity have been found to spend less time going over material and their questions are answered correctly the first time, allowing more time for instruction. Clarity is a complex behaviour because it is related to many other cognitive behaviours such as the content, familiarity with the material, and delivery strategies (eg whether the teacher uses a discussion, direct instruction or lecture approach, question-and-answer, or small-group techniques). Nevertheless, research shows that both the cognitive clarity and oral clarity of presentations vary substantially among teachers. This in turn produces differences in pupil performance on cognitive tests of achievement (Borich, 1996).

Achievement is increased when the teacher not only actively presents the material, but does so in a structured way, such as by beginning with an overview and/or review of objectives. Effective teachers tend to outline the content to be covered and signal transitions between lesson parts. Attention is drawn to the most important ideas, and subparts of the lesson are summarised as it proceeds. The main ideas are reviewed at the end of the lesson. In this way, the information is not only better remembered by the pupils, but is also more easily apprehended as an integrated whole, with recognition of the relationship between the parts. It is also important to explain not just how, but why, procedures work (Brophy & Good, 1986; Lampert, 1988).

Pupil achievement has been found to be higher when information is presented with a certain amount of redundancy, particularly in the form of repeating and reviewing general rules and key concepts. Information needs to be presented with a high degree of clarity and enthusiasm. As far as pacing goes, the research suggests that for younger pupils and for basic skills, a brisk pace which helps to maintain lesson momentum and attention has been found to be most effective, while for older pupils, or where teachers have to make more abstract presentations of more complex and abstract subject matter, it may be necessary to move at a slower pace to allow more time for understanding to develop (Brophy & Good, 1986; Good, Grouws & Ebmeier, 1983; Lampert, 1988; Walberg, 1986).

This focus on the teacher presenting material in an active way to pupils should, however, not be equated to a traditional 'lecturing and drill' approach in which the pupils remain passive. Active teachers ask a lot of questions (more than other teachers), and involve pupils in class discussion. In this way, pupils are kept involved in the lesson and the teacher has the chance to monitor children's understanding of the concepts taught. Individual work is only assigned after the teacher has made sure pupils have grasped the material sufficiently to be ready for it. In general, effective teachers have been found to teach a concept, then ask questions to test children's understanding, and if the material did not seem well understood, to re-teach the

Lesson clarity is central to teaching thinking. Pupils should know what they are doing and why.

In teaching thinking information is broken into manageable chunks, but the relationship between these pieces is also emphasised.

Active presentation is a key feature of teaching thinking lessons.

concept, followed by more monitoring. Teachers must provide clear feedback to pupils resulting from either pupils' questions or answers to teacher questions (Brophy & Good, 1986; Good, Grouws & Ebmeier, 1983; Brophy, 1986). One of the main purposes of a Strategy like **Living Graphs** and **Fortune Lines** is for the teacher to have opportunities to do this. This kind of formative assessment is essential of effective teaching (Tunstall & Gipps, 1996; Black & Wiliam, 1998).

To summarise, the research literature suggests the effective teacher:

- informs learners of the lesson objectives (eg describes what behaviours will be tested or required on future assignments as a result of the lesson): we would add that the pupils have to understand such objectives;
- provides learners with an organising structure (eg places the lesson in a perspective of past and/or future lesson): sometimes described as 'activating prior knowledge';
- checks for prior learning relevant to the task at beginning of lesson (eg determines level of understanding of prerequisite facts or concepts and re-teaches if necessary);
- gives directives clearly and distinctly (eg repeats directives when needed or divides them into smaller pieces): 'chunking learning';
- knows the current attainment levels of pupils and teaches at or slightly above learners' current level of functioning (eg knows the pupils and how to pitch the content of a lesson): provides an appropriate level of challenge;
- uses examples, illustrations, and demonstrations to explain and clarify (eg uses visual props to help interpret and reinforce main points);
- provides a review or summary at end of each lesson: longer tem goals of motivating learners and creating a learning disposition needs to involve pupils in discussing and evaluating their own learning.

Our experience in teaching thinking has highlighted some of the tensions in applying such behavioural pointers in developing effective teaching. One group of teachers moved from a focus on debriefing in their analysis of their teaching to the importance of introductions, or 'launching' of activities. They identified that there is a tension between 'clarity of instruction' and 'checking for prior learning' which can alter the precise focus of what needs to be taught. You can't be entirely clear about what you are going to do, if what you do depends on the pupils' responses. The management of teaching thinking strategies is powerful in eliciting some feedback from the pupils, rather than relying on direct instruction. However, the skill lies in the management of the task and in signalling clearly to pupils what is significant in the lesson and what can lead to success.

2. Instructional variety

This key behaviour refers to the variability or flexibility of delivery during the presentation of a lesson. For example, it might include the planned mixture of different classroom approaches or techniques. Research indicates increased pupil achievement from the use of variety in instructional materials and techniques, the frequency and variety of reinforcement used, and types of feedback given to pupils (Brophy & Good, 1986). Effectiveness is therefore the appropriate choice of approach to match a particular context. This is not the same as teaching to particular learning styles. Our interpretation of the research in this area is that teaching with varied approaches is beneficial for all pupils, not that teaching visually supports particular visual learners or that kinaesthetic approaches support (only) kinaesthetic learners. Also knowing that instructional variety is important does not help you decide how and when to vary the instruction!

> Presenting ideas and material in different forms provides variety and reinforces the key points in different ways.

Teachers' questions

One of the most effective ways of creating variety during instruction is to ask questions. Many different types of questions can be asked, and when integrated into the pacing and sequencing of a lesson, they create meaningful variation (Kerry, 1982; Brown & Wragg, 1993). Therefore, the effective teacher needs to know the art of asking questions and how to discriminate among different question formats: fact questions; process questions; convergent questions; divergent questions. This teacher also responds to pupils' answers so as to incorporate them into the discussion and open up opportunities for greater pupil participation (Dillon, 1994).

Dillon (1994) suggests a range of alternatives to questioning, what he terms 'non-question moves'. These are designed to act as a model of exemplary discussion behaviours for pupils for the way they should talk in a discussion. In reviewing the strategies Dillon suggests that in general, following a contribution to the discussion on the question under consideration, the other participants have four broad choices, each with several specifics to choose from: they can ask a question about what the speaker has said; make a statement in relation to what the speaker has just said; give a signal of receiving what the speaker is saying; maintain an attentive silence. In using these strategies Dillon argues that the teacher's lead and example will be helpful to the pupils in modelling and fostering appropriate discussion behaviour and in encouraging pupil questions. Therefore participants in this kind of classroom discourse have five broad choices: teacher questions; pupil questions; statements; signals; and silences.

> Alternatives to questioning are important techniques.

Similarly, Wood (1992) suggests that in order for pupils to take the initiative, the balance of control needs to be shifted in their direction, the achievement of which demands attention to a teacher's use of questions and alternative conversational tactics to a lecturing approach. His alternative discourse strategies involve 'low control' moves from teachers whereby instead of asking frequent questions they give their own thought and ideas in which they speculate, surmise, interpret, illustrate, or simply listen and acknowledge what pupils have to say. These alternatives to teacher questions which include telling, suggesting, negotiating and listening are designed to free pupils to give their own views, to reveal their knowledge and uncertainties, and to seek information and explanation through questions of their own. Once the pupils have helped to shape the verbal agenda, teacher questions are more likely to involve a genuine attempt to explore their knowledge and ideas. One of the most powerful features of teaching thinking lessons is the way in which patterns of discourse alter as the Strategies and Approaches are used.

> Teaching thinking activities seek to open up space for articulation and discussion.

Nystrand & Gamoran (1991) advocate that teachers pay more attention to the way in which they evaluate pupil responses so that there is more 'high-level evaluation' whereby teachers incorporate pupils' answers into subsequent questions. In this process called *uptake*, many of the teacher's questions are seen as being *authentic* in that they are shaped by what immediately precedes them. This is in contrast to recitation where there is usually a prepared list of *test* questions with pre-specified answers from a list of 'essential' information and knowledge against which a pupil's knowledge can be checked. It is suggested that through this process teachers can engage pupils in a probing and extended discussion in which they signal to them their interest in what they think and not just whether they know and can report what someone else thinks or has said. Therefore, when *high level evaluation* and *uptake* occur the teacher ratifies the importance of a pupils' response and allows it to modify or affect the course of the discussion in some way. Thus the responses are incorporated into an unfolding exchange which links together teacher questions and pupil responses so that it takes on a conversation-like quality in which the linkages contribute to the coherence.

> In the **Community of Enquiry** pupils are expected to develop 'uptake' of *each others'* responses.

Another helpful behaviour is 'probing' (Borich, 1996). Probing refers to a teacher's statements that encourage pupils to elaborate upon an answer, either their own or another pupil's. Probing may take the form of a general question or can include other expressions that elicit clarification of an answer, solicit additional information about a response, or redirect a pupil's response in a more fruitful direction. Probing is often used to shift a discussion to some higher thought level. Effective teachers have been found to ask more 'process' questions (those that call for explanations by the pupils), though the majority of questions asked were still 'product' questions (those that call for a single, easily evaluated, response) (Brophy & Good, 1986, Good & Brophy, 1991).

> Probing responses positively helps check for understanding. This is part of mediation.

Feedback to learners is important. If pupils give an incorrect response, the teacher should indicate this. This can be done in the form of a simple negation, and not in the form of personal criticism (except when the failure to answer was clearly the result of inattention or lack of effort). Personal criticism of the pupils should be avoided as, if wrong answers elicit such responses, pupils, especially the less confident and able, will be reluctant to participate in class discussion or offer solutions. This should be avoided. The teacher should rephrase the incorrectly answered question or give clues to attempt to enable the pupil to answer it correctly. If this does not succeed, the question should be turned over to another pupil. It can

> Effective feedback is at the heart of effective teaching.

be important when the right answer is found to explain why this answer is right, and also why the previous one was incorrect. In general, effective teachers have been found to provide more feedback than less effective teachers (Brophy & Good, 1986; Black & Wiliam, 1998).

Questioning and modelling by pupils is a valuable Strategy.

Dillon's (1994) work suggests that pupils should be encouraged to ask questions (as long as they are not intended to waste time). These questions should be redirected to the class before being answered by other pupils or the teacher, and relevant comments by pupils should be incorporated into the lesson, especially as for older pupils or those more experienced at contributing ideas. Overall, it is clear that effective teaching is not only active, but interactive (Brophy & Good, 1986; Nystrand & Gamoran, 1991). The **Community of Enquiry** Approach develops such effective behaviours at class level.

Variety in teaching and learning style is also associated with learning gains: active, interactive whole class teaching and co-operative small group work have their merits, and the amount of time to be spent on both should depend on factors such as pupil age, ability and, most crucially, the task to be performed or the subject to be learned (Galton *et al*, 1980; Mortimore et al, 1988; Bennett & Dunne, 1992). Teaching thinking Strategies offer a source for such instructional variety. **Odd One Out** in particular is a valuable technique to add some zest to the beginning or end of a lesson, as well as offering powerful formative feedback for the teacher.

Effective classroom talk

There is considerable evidence that most lessons in schools usually follow a similar discourse pattern (Edwards & Westgate, 1994). This is described variously as 'Initiate-Respond-Evaluate' (I-R-E) or 'Initiate-Respond-Feedback' (I-R-F) from Sinclair & Coulthard's (1975 and 1992) descriptions of moves and acts. One of the possible reasons for this type of discourse structure is that the class teacher is clearly in control of both the content and turn taking in any classroom discussion. It is easier to manage and maintain control. In addition it may promote effective transmission of information, though pupils are encouraged mainly to recall information (Edwards & Westgate, 1994 p156). Thinking skills programmes advocate a less directive role for the teacher and encourage mediation or scaffolding of pupil's thinking. This could be interpreted as providing a structure for what Westgate & Hughes (1989) recommend in creating 'more space' for pupils in classroom interaction. Because of the difficulties of managing the turn-taking of a large numbers of pupils, some observers (Barnes & Todd, 1977/1995; Edwards & Furlong, 1978, Edwards & Mercer, 1987; Edwards & Westgate, 1994) have advocated the use of collaborative group work as a way of 'decentralizing' classroom communication so as to encourage more pupils to participate in and practice forms of academic discourse normally dominated by the teacher. Some teachers and researchers (eg Phillips, 1985; Reid *et al*, 1989; Berrill, 1990; Maybin, 1991) have even explored the possibilities of teacher-less discussion as an alternative to whole class recitation. We would argue that teaching thinking offers other ways to structure classroom interaction that are also worth exploring.

In teaching thinking activities pupils 'articulate' their thinking. Literally this means that 'they join it up' through their talk.

Many teaching thinking activities involve paired or small-group work as part of the lesson structure.

In discussing the features of group work where pupils are encouraged to explore meanings collaboratively, Edwards & Westgate (1994) and Barnes & Todd (1995) point out the clear differences in discourse structure between this and whole class instruction. Because the absence of the teacher means there is no authoritative figure to dominate the discourse, there are no clearly marked asymmetrical relationships and the consequent lack of pre-allocated rights makes it necessary for the pupils to negotiate the terms of their interaction as they go along. As Edwards (1980) argues, turn-taking is managed locally and interactionally in such group discussion and it sets up different expectations and patterns of working because speakers potentially have equal rights and joint ownership of the interaction. The patterns of interaction are therefore strikingly different from the kinds of discourse associated with the whole-class or transmission model of teaching. Therefore there are frequent overlaps and a lack of pauses as it is usually not clear until the moment of decision who will enter and who will control the up-coming turn. Each pupil's contribution is also closely contingent on the contributions of others and necessitates close listening to what has gone before. The absence of an authoritative figure in the conversation also means that there is no one to evaluate responses so pupils have to pool their responses to draw their own conclusions or refine their responses. It also allows for an interplay of alternative frames, and, because power is distributed amongst the pupils, they have a greater opportunity to initiate questions, to evaluate each other's responses, and to control the discourse for their own purposes.

In this way, as Edwards & Mercer (1987) suggest, pupils can share in and practice forms of academic discourse in the classroom normally dominated by the teacher: that is, sharing, comparing, contrasting and arguing from different perspectives, providing opportunities for 'instructional conversation' or the 'shared construction or negotiation of meaning'. Therefore pupils are given more opportunities to develop linguistically and cognitively in the discourse structure of collaborative group work. Cazden (1988) also argues that collaborative group work has a justifiable role on the grounds that it is *'The only (our emphasis) context in which children can reverse interactional roles with the same intellectual content, giving directions as well as following them, and asking questions as well as answering them, is with their peers.'* We would partially disagree with this, arguing that the discourse in a class experienced in using the **Community of Enquiry** Approach has many of the features of collaborative group discourse but operating on a whole class scale. Further our experience of the role of the teacher as mediator in teaching thinking lessons suggests that these types of exchanges can be teacher/pupil as well as pupil/pupil.

> Changes to the discourse structure are part of why we believe teaching thinking works. These changes occur in both small-group work and whole class approaches such as the **Community of Enquiry**.

Wells (1993) suggests teachers can make different use of the feedback move in the recitation (I-R-F) cycle beyond the evaluative move for checking pupils' knowledge. He argues that the third move can be used to extend the pupil's answer, to draw out its significance, or to make connections with other parts of the pupil's total experience during lesson topics so as to create a greater equality of participation. Such episodes are marked by *'common points of reference'* where everyone had *'relevant personal experience of the shared activities from which to construct common knowledge'* (p 30). Therefore, teachers can provide extending rather than evaluating feedback so that *'it is in this third step in the co-construction of meaning that the next cycle of the learning-and-teaching spiral has its point of departure'* (p 35).

> Extending answers through feedback and making connections is 'teaching for transfer'.

Bennett & Dunne (1992) and Galton & Williamson (1992) argue that successful group work only occurs when pupils are made aware of the purpose of the task, and the skills and behaviours that are essential for its effective operation. They strongly advocate training in group-work skills: for example, this might entail knowledge of how to listen, to question or challenge within a group discussion. They also emphasise the need for teachers to make their expectations explicit through clear 'ground rules' so that the pupils realise the importance teachers attach to such behaviours. By emphasising and encouraging such co-operative effort, and by providing feedback about the gains, Bennett & Dunne suggest pupils will perceive the value and benefits of talking and collaborative group work.

> Teaching thinking makes aims explicit and debriefs both the process of learning as well as the curriculum outcomes.

Research suggests effective teachers know how to blend individual, small group and whole class teaching successfully. Thus, for the teaching of basic skills or factual knowledge, active whole class teaching is clearly the most effective strategy, though practice or assessment of concepts taught might fruitfully incorporate some small group work. For example, mathematical problem solving and thinking skills are probably best enhanced through collaborative small group work, although an element of whole class teaching will be needed to explain the task and to teach the pupils the skills necessary to do collaborative group work (Peterson, 1988; Hembree, 1992; Stevens & Slavin, 1995). All in all, the research literature suggests that the question is not whether to do whole class teaching or small group work, but how to do them both, in a blended fashion (Galton & Williamson, 1992; Barnes & Todd, 1995; Galton, 1995). It seems likely that teaching practice which blends teacher-led approaches with group work and paired work will produce the highest learning gains (Croll & Moses, 1988; Johnson & Johnson, 1990; Pollard *et al*, 1994).

To summarise, the research literature suggests the effective teacher:

- uses attention-gaining devices (eg begins with a challenging question, visual prop or practical example): David Leat describes this as 'launching' a teaching thinking lesson;
- shows enthusiasm and animation through variation in eye contact, voice and gestures (eg changes pitch and volume, moves about during transitions to new activity);
- varies modes of presentation (eg lectures, asks questions, then regularly provides opportunities for independent practice);
- uses a mix of rewards and reinforcement (eg verbal praise, independent study etc);

- incorporates pupil ideas or participation in some aspects of the instruction (eg develops 'uptake' or uses indirect instruction or divergent questioning);
- varies types of questions and statements (eg divergent, convergent, and probes; eg to clarify, to solicit, to redirect);
- uses an appropriate blend of whole class, group-based and individual teaching.

> Infusion develops thinking skills strategies across the curriculum, but in specific subjects. The task structure ensures that discussion quickly focuses on the subject content.

3. Teacher task orientation

This effective behaviour refers to how much classroom time the teacher devotes to the task of teaching an academic subject: the time actually spent teaching. The more time dedicated to the task of teaching a specific topic, the greater the opportunity pupils have to learn. Most researchers agree that pupil performance is higher in classrooms with teachers who spent the majority of their time teaching subject-specific content as opposed to devoting large amounts of time to the organisational processes and materials that may be needed to acquire the content. It follows that classrooms in which teacher-pupil interactions focus more on intellectual content than on procedural issues (such as how to use materials or classroom rules and organisational procedures) are more likely to have higher rates of achievement (Brophy & Good, 1986; Hafner, 1993; Herman & Klein, 1996).

To summarise, the research literature suggests the effective teacher:

- develops medium and short term lesson plans that reflect the most relevant features of the curriculum;
- stops or prevents interruptions with minimum of classroom disruption (eg has pre-established academic and work rules to 'protect' intrusions into instructional time);
- handles administrative and clerical interruptions efficiently (eg giving out of materials) by anticipating some tasks and deferring others to non-instructional time);
- chooses the most appropriate teaching strategy for the objectives being taught (eg uses direct instruction for knowledge and literal comprehension objectives and group work or indirect instruction for inquiry and problem-solving objectives);
- has effective feedback to pupils built in (eg weekly and monthly reviews, feedback, and testing sessions).

> One of the commonest responses by teachers who adopt teaching thinking approaches is that pupils' engagement in learning tasks improves.

4. Engagement in the learning process

This key behaviour refers to the amount of learning time devoted to an academic subject and is one of the most recently researched teacher behaviours related to pupil performance (eg Brophy & Good, 1986; Hafner, 1993; Herman & Klein, 1996). It is related to a teacher's task orientation and to content coverage, thereby providing pupils with the greatest opportunity to learn the material to be assessed.

Being given the 'opportunity to learn' is clearly related to such factors as length of the school day and year, and to the amount of hours devoted to each subject. It is, however, also related to the quality of classroom management, especially to what is known as 'time on task' (ie the amount of time pupils are actively engaged in learning activities in the classroom, as opposed to socialising etc). In teaching thinking the bridging between formal and informal learning, the valuing of pupils' experiences and the intrinsic motivation of the tasks all contribute to increased engagement.

> Teaching thinking activities usually have a range of possible successful outcomes.

5. Pupil success rate

A crucial aspect of the research on teaching time and pupil engagement has been the level of difficulty of the material presented. In these studies, level of difficulty was measured by the rate at which pupils understood and correctly completed exercises. The three levels of difficulty are as follows:

1. high success, in which the pupil understands the task and makes only occasional errors;
2. moderate success, in which the pupil has partial understanding but some substantive errors;

3. low success, in which the pupil does not understand the task.

Findings suggest that a teacher's task orientation (actual teaching time) and pupil engagement are closely related to pupil success rate. Instruction that produces a moderate-to-high success rate results in increased performance because more content is covered at the learner's current level of understanding. This applies not only to expository or didactic forms of instruction in basic academic skills, but to thinking skills instruction. Research has also shown that instruction that promotes low error rate (high success) can contribute to increased levels of self-esteem and to positive attitudes toward the subject matter and the school (Slavin *et al*, 1996).

Subject specific issues

Whilst there are teaching factors that are functional in generating high gain across all curriculum areas, a review of research by Borich (1996) also suggests that there is a degree of 'subject specificity' in what makes a difference. For example, in the teaching of mathematics, effective instruction includes the use of differentiated materials, whole class interactive instruction and the limiting of unguided or independent work, whereas in the teaching of reading it includes discussing, explaining, and questioning to stimulate cognitive processes and promote learner responses. Mortimore *et al* (1988) also show subject difference with the regular use of tests showing gains in mathematics but having a negative effect upon reading. We speculate that this is due to the feedback that pupils get from the nature of the subject material. In mathematics, there are correct answers to calculations and equations. It is unhelpful to practice lots of examples independently whilst applying an algorithm incorrectly and not realising this until the SATs! Formative feedback from tests can therefore be incorporated into a mastery approach to learning in mathematics where mistakes help you learn. Short feedback loops are essential. In English, it is less easy to judge that the content of your writing is 'correct' so you need to know what makes your writing better which involves modelling, scaffolding and discussion, rather than a test which does not help you improve. Understanding the criteria for assessment in both subjects is more crucial.

Teaching for high attainment

Borich (1996) in a review of classroom research into behaviours which promote the most achievement amongst pupils from low and high socio-economic status (SES) groups suggests the following approaches. We believe his approach dangerously misidentifies SES as a proxy for attainment, and creates assumptions about pupils' potential according to their background, but his findings have some relevance and so are reported here. For lower-SES (or, if we are correct, for lower attaining) pupils he claims teachers need to:

> We believe that 'attainment' is a more useful term than 'ability' and believe that low attaining pupils can become higher attaining with teaching thinking Approaches.

- provide a warm and encouraging classroom climate by letting pupils know help is available;
- encourage an initial response from a pupil, however crude, before moving to the next pupil;
- present material in small pieces, with opportunities to practice what has been learned after each piece;
- emphasise knowledge and applications before teaching patterns and abstractions (ie present most concrete learning first);
- monitor each pupil's progress at regular intervals (eg by using progress charts to help record improvement);
- help pupils who need help immediately (eg using peer and cross-age tutors, if necessary);
- minimise disruptions by maintaining structure and flow between activities (eg by organising and planning transitions in advance);
- supplement standard curriculum with specialised materials to meet the needs of individual pupils (eg by using different media, learning resources, and the personal experience of pupils to promote interest and attention).

And for higher-SES pupils (or, as we would see it, to ensure high attainment for all pupils):

- check right answers by requiring extended reasoning;
- pose questions that require associations, generalisations, and inferences;
- encourage pupils to use this same level of questioning;
- supplement the curriculum with challenging material, some of which is slightly above pupils' current level of attainment;
- encourage pupil-to-pupil and pupil-to-teacher interactions in which learners take responsibility for evaluating their own learning;
- actively encourage pupils in verbal questions and answers that go beyond text and workbook content.

Teacher affect or emotions, in which teachers convey their enthusiasm to pupils in many ways, the most common being vocal inflections, gestures, eye contact and animation, is believed to be important in promoting pupil engagement in the learning process, particularly amongst lower-SES classes. Borich argues that four of the approaches shown for lower-SES classrooms (pupil responses, over-teaching/over-learning, classroom interaction individualisation) can be seen as special ways of creating pupil engagement with high rates of success. Also, frequently correcting wrong answers in the absence of warmth or encouragement could be construed as personal criticism by the less confident pupil, who already may have a poor self concept. Therefore, feedback that could be construed as criticism may need to occur in the context of a more consistently warmer and encouraging environment than may be needed for the more confident learner. Or, to put it another way, feedback needs to take into account the quality of the relationship between teacher and learner. In addition, activities such as discussion and problem-solving may require more structure (and preparation) for different learners with different experience of success and failure.

> Teaching thinking improves the quality of teaching and learning relationships in the classroom.

Review of important teacher effectiveness indicators

In summarising the general indicators of effective teaching that are currently supported by the research literature, the effective teacher:

- takes personal responsibility for pupil learning and has positive expectations for every learner;
- matches the difficulty of the lesson with the ability level of the pupils, and varies the difficulty when necessary to attain high success rates;
- gives pupils the opportunity to practice newly learned concepts and to receive timely feedback on their performance;
- maximises teaching time to increase what is covered and to give pupils the greatest opportunity to learn;
- provides direction and control of pupil learning through questioning, structuring and probing;
- uses a variety of teaching materials and verbal and visual aids to foster use of pupils' ideas and engagement in the learning process;
- elicits responses from pupils each time a question is asked before moving to the next pupil or question;
- presents material in small steps when necessary with opportunities to practise;
- encourages pupils to reason and elaborate on correct answers;
- engages pupils in verbal questions and answers;
- uses naturally occurring classroom dialogue to get pupils to elaborate, extend and comment on the context being learned;
- gradually shifts some of the responsibility for learning to the pupils – encouraging independent thinking, problem solving and decision making through collaborative group work;
- provides learners with mental strategies for organising and learning the content being taught.

Review of teaching thinking principles

We believe that these behaviours closely map onto the principles of teaching thinking we advocated in the *Introduction*:

Clear purpose

The purposes of tasks are made explicit as part of the teaching process and these aims are, at least in part, understood by pupils. This helps to provide pupils with specific targets that they can achieve and can reflect on. This means helping pupils to understand not just *what* they have to do, but *why* they are doing it.

Articulation

Pupils talk about their work and are encouraged to describe and articulate their thinking. This has several benefits. From the teacher's point of view, you get a chance to see how pupils are thinking as they explain their reasoning. This is an opportunity to address any misconceptions or develop their thinking. For the pupils, talking is usually seen as 'easy', but they get the chance to change their minds in the light of what others say.

Mediation

The teacher intervenes to discuss the learning that is taking place (and perhaps involves pupils in this through modelling and collaborative work). In this way the teacher 'mediates' the learning. This includes whole class explanation and discussion as well as direct teaching.

Connecting learning

The teacher and pupils make connections both within the tasks, between tasks and with their wider experience. This is sometimes described as 'bridging' of learning by the teacher or 'transfer' of learning for pupils.

Evaluation

Pupils evaluate their own performance. Only once learning objectives are meaningfully understood, can pupils start to evaluate how successful they have been and then identify why they were successful or unsuccessful.

Metacognition

The teacher and pupils discuss and evaluate the learning that has taken place. This supports pupils in seeing themselves as successful learners and able to learn rather than just accepting that they are either good at it or not. It also helps to develop an understanding of learning strategies, styles or approaches that may help them in future learning.

Obviously, teaching involves a sense of timing, sequencing and pacing that cannot be conveyed by any list of behaviours. It is the thinking and intention that connects these behaviours together that is important to the effective teacher, giving each its proper emphasis in the context of the classroom. It is the combination of curriculum, learning objectives, teaching materials and diverse learners that provides the decision-making context. It also points to the need for coaching and feedback to go hand-in-hand with teachers' professional development. Observation schedules to record teacher-pupil interactions can provide a useful tool for professional development as they allow for supportive discussion by groups of teachers of data derived from their own classrooms. Action research where classroom data is used to test out the findings of other research can also be a powerful means to bring about change. Developing teaching so that effective behaviours become more prevalent in teaching is a challenging agenda. *Our experience suggests that these behaviours develop under the umbrella of teaching thinking.* It clusters together the teaching approach or pedagogical strategy, the specific curriculum or subject objectives and content and the teaching and learning interactions between teacher and pupil and between pupil and pupil. It is this clustering which makes it so powerful.

> Effective teaching is about making effective choices in complex situations.

> The Strategies in teaching thinking provide a structure to support teachers by providing diagnostic information and space to make more effective choices.

References

Askew M., Brown M., Rhodes V., Johnson D. & Wiliam D.
(1997) *Effective Teachers of Numeracy Final Report* London: King's College

Aubrey C.
(1997) *Mathematics Teaching in the Early Years: an Investigation of Teachers' Subject Knowledge* London: Falmer Press

Barnes D. & Todd F.
(1977) *Communication and Learning in Small Groups*, London: Routledge and Kegan Paul

Barnes D. & Todd F.
(1995) *Communication and Learning Revisited: Making Meaning Through Talk* Portsmouth, NH: Heinemann

Bennett N. & Dunne E.
(1992) *Managing Classroom Groups* Hemel Hempstead: Simon and Schuster

Berrill D.
(1990) 'Adolescents arguing' in Wilkinson A., Davies A. & Berrill D. *Spoken English Illuminated* Milton Keynes: Open University Press

Black P. & Wiliam D.
(1998) 'Assessment and Classroom Learning' in *Assessment in Education 5.1*

Borich G.
(1996) *Effective Teaching Methods* (3rd Edition) New York: Macmillan

Brophy J.
(1986) 'Teaching and Learning Mathematics: Where Research Should Be Going' in *Journal for Research in Mathematics Education* New York: Macmillan

Brophy J. & Good T.L.
(1986) 'Teacher Behaviour and Student Achievement' in Wittrock M.C. (ed) *Handbook of Research on Teaching* New York: Macmillan

Brown G.A. & Wragg E.C.
(1993) *Questioning* London: Routledge

Brown S. & McIntyre D.
(1993) *Making Sense of Teaching* Milton Keynes: Open University Press

Cazden C.B.
(1988) *Classroom Discourse: The Language of Teaching and Learning* Portsmouth, NH: Heinemann

Croll P. & Moses D.
(1988) 'Teaching Methods and Time on Task in Junior Classrooms' in *Educational Researcher 30*, 2 pp 90-97

Dillon J.T.
(1988) *Questioning and Teaching: A Manual of Practice* London: Crook Helm

Dillon J.T.
(1994) *Using Discussion in Classrooms* Buckingham: Open University Press

Edwards A.D.
(1980) 'Patterns of Power and Authority in Classroom Talk' in Woods P. (ed) *Teacher Strategies* London: Crook Helm

Edwards A.D. & Furlong V.J.
(1978) *The Language of Teaching* London: Heinemann

Edwards A.D. & Westgate D.P.G.
(1994) (2nd Edition) *Investigating Classroom Talk* London: The Falmer Press

Edwards D. & Mercer N.
(1987) *Common Knowledge: The Development of Understanding in the Classroom* London: Methuen

Elliott J.
(1996) 'School Effectiveness Research and its Critics: Alternative Visions of Schooling' in *Cambridge Journal of Education 26* pp199-224

Galton M., Simon B. & Croll P.
(1980) *Inside the Primary Classroom* London: Routledge

Galton M. & Williamson J.
(1992) *Group Work in the Primary Classroom* London: Routledge and Kegan Paul

Galton M.
(1995) *Crisis in the Primary Classroom* London: David Fulton

Galton M., Hargreaves L., Comber C., Wall D. & Pell A.
(1999) *Inside the Primary Classroom: 20 Years On* London: Routledge

Tunstall P. & Gipps C.
(1996) 'Teacher Feedback to Young Children in Formative Assessment: a Typology' in *British Educational Research Journal 22,4* pp 389-404

Good T. & Brophy J.
(1991) *Looking in Classrooms* New York: Harper Collins

Good T.L., Grouws D.A. & Ebmeier H.
(1983) *Active Mathematics Teaching* New York: Longman

Hafner A.L.
(1993) 'Teaching-Method Scales and Mathematics-Class Achievement: What Works With Different Outcomes?' in *American Educational Research Journal 30, 1* pp 71 - 94

Hembree R.
(1992) 'Experiments and Relational Studies in Problem Solving: Meta-Analysis' in *Journal for Research in Mathematics Education 23, 3* pp 242-273

Herman J.L. & Klein C.D.
(1996) 'Evaluating Equity in Alternative Assessment: An Illustration of Opportunity-to-learn' in *Journal of Educational Research 89, 4* pp246-256

Johnson D.W. & Johnson R.T.
(1990) 'Co-operative Learning and Achievement' in Sharan S. (ed.) *Co-operative Learning: Theory and Research* New York: Praeger

Kerry T.
(1982) *Effective Questioning* Basingstoke: Macmillan

Lampert M.
(1988) 'What Can Research on Teacher Education Tell Us About Improving Quality in Mathematics Education?' in *Teaching and Teacher Education 4, 2* pp 157-170

Leat D.
(1993) 'Competence, Teaching, Thinking and Feeling' in *Oxford Review of Education 19,4* pp 499-510

Maybin J.
(1991) 'Children's Informal Talk and the Construction of Meaning' in *English in Education 25, 2* pp34- 49

Mortimore P., Sammons P., Stoll L., Lewis D. & Ecob R.
(1988) *School Matters* Wells: Open Books

Moseley D., Higgins S., Bramald R., Hardman F., Miller J., Mroz M., Tse H., Newton D., Thompson I., Williamson J., Halligan J., Bramald S., Newton L., Tymms P., Henderson B. & Stout J.
(1999) *Ways Forward with ICT: Effective Pedagogy using Information and Communications Technology in Literacy and Numeracy in Primary Schools* Newcastle: University of Newcastle upon Tyne

Nystrand M. & Gamoran A.
(1991) 'Student Engagement: When Recitation Becomes Conversation' in Waxman H.C. & Walberg H.J. (eds) *Effective Teaching: Current Research* Berkley, CA: McCutchan

Peterson P.L.
(1988) 'Teaching for Higher Order Thinking in Mathematics: The Challenge for the Next Decade' in Grouws D.A., Cooney T.J., & Jones D. (eds) *Perspectives on Research on Effective Mathematics Teaching* Reston, VA: NCTM

Phillips T.
(1985) 'Beyond Lip-service: Discourse Development After the Age of Nine' in Wells G. & Nicholls J. (eds) in *Language and Learning* Lewes: The Falmer Press

Pollard A.
(1985) *The Social World of the Primary School* London: Cassell

Pollard A., Broadfoot P., Croll P., Osborne N. & Abbott D.
(1994) *Changing English Primary Schools?* London: Cassell

Reid J., Forrestal P. & Cook J.
(1989) *Small Group Learning in the Classroom* Scarborough: Chalkface Press

Slavin R.E., Madden N.A., Karweit N.L., Dolan L., & Wasik B.A.
(1996) *Every Child, Every School: Success for All* Newbury Park, CA: Corwin

Stevens R.J. & Slavin R.E.
(1995) 'The Co-operative Elementary School: Effects on Students' Achievement, Attitudes and Social Relations' in *American Educational Research Journal 32, 2* pp321-351

Schulman L.S.
(1986) 'Those Who Understand: Knowledge Growth in Teaching'in *Educational Researcher 15* pp 4-14

Sinclair J.McH. & Coulthard R.M.
(1975) *Towards an Analysis of Discourse: The English Used By Teachers and Pupils* London: Oxford University Press

Sinclair J. & Coulthard M.
(1992) 'Towards an Analysis of Discourse' in Coulthard M. (ed) *Advances in Spoken Discourse Analysis* London: Routledge

Walberg H.J.
(1986) 'Syntheses of Research on Teaching' in Wittrock M.C. (ed) *Handbook of Research on Teaching* New York: Macmillan

Wells G.
(1993) 'Re-evaluating the IRF Sequence: A Proposal for the Articulation of Theories of Activity and Discourse for the Analysis of Teaching and Learning in the Classroom in *Linguistics and Education 5* pp 1-37

Westgate D & Hughes M.
(1989) 'Nursery Nurses as Talk Partners' in *Education 3-1, 17,2* pp 54-58

Wood D.
(1992) 'Teaching Talk' in Norman K. (ed) *Thinking Voices: The Work of the National Oracy Project* London: Hodder and Stoughton

Wood D.
(1998) *How Children Think and Learn* (Second edition) Oxford: Blackwell

Wragg E.C.
(1993) *Primary Teaching Skills* London: Routledge

12
Making it work: effective professional development

'We know only too well the sorry spectacle of the teacher who, in the ordinary schoolroom, must pour certain cut and dried facts into the heads of the scholars. In order to succeed in this barren task, she finds it necessary to discipline her pupils into immobility and to force their attention. Prizes and punishments are ever-ready and efficient aids to the master who must force into a given attitude of mind and body those who are condemned to be listeners.'

Maria Montessori *The Montessori Method (1912)*

12 Making it work: effective professional development

This chapter describes how teaching thinking has developed in the North East of England and identifies some of the hurdles and challenges in using teaching thinking as a means of effective professional development and raising attainment. We do not have any easy solutions that guarantee success. Each classroom and each school is different and faces slightly different issues. Our particular experience in the North East of England suggests that it is possible to be successful in a wide range of settings and situations but that there are a number of important issues to consider.

Developments in the North East

The teaching thinking movement in the North East of England started with small numbers and groups of interested teachers. They used published programmes and books of ideas as starting points for practical classroom activities. This developed into a network of schools and teachers supported by the team at Newcastle University (NETS - North East Thinking Skills). Development work on some of the particular Strategies described in this book was pioneered by David Leat and a group of secondary geography teachers which led to the publication of *Thinking Through Geography* (1998). As our knowledge of the issues in implementing published programmes developed we focused on an action research model developed by Viv Baumfield through courses offered as part of a Masters in Education. These courses alone have involved over 200 teachers and the NETS network involves several hundred schools, from tiny rural first schools, to large urban comprehensives. The work has also been supported significantly by some Local Education Authority advisers. Most notable is the work achieved in Northumberland where Mel Rockett has enthusiastically promoted teaching thinking, or 'Thinking for Learning' as it has evolved, to encompass a wide range of ideas, strategies and techniques. Almost every school in Northumberland seems to have been involved in some way. Success has also been achieved in Sunderland, through Jane Duffy, and North Tyneside through Bruce Macfarlane. This partnership approach has been one of the most exciting (though, at times, frustrating!) aspects of the developments in the North East. It has led to the development of a New Opportunities Fund ICT course 'Thinking Through Literacy Numeracy and Science' offered by GridREF 2000 under the government's ICT training courses for serving teachers in partnership with five local LEAs. This course looks at how ICT can support teachers' preparation and presentation of teaching thinking materials as well as activities where pupils use ICT in their learning. National interest is reflected in the Teacher Training Agency funded North East School Based Research Consortium and has led to the trialling and establishment of a series of teacher research scholarships in teaching thinking funded by the National Union of Teachers.

> The work on teaching thinking in the North East has been a partnership between the Thinking Skills Research Centre at the University of Newcastle, local teachers, schools and LEAs.

Locus of control

Of significance was the enthusiasm for teaching thinking generated by the individual teachers. This was sparked by the feedback they received in their classrooms as they tried out ideas and activities. Enthusiasm spread as teachers talked to each other about their classroom experiences. As the momentum of interest grew it started to involve whole schools where the heads and staff chose 'teaching thinking' and 'thinking for learning' as their focus for professional development. At primary level we also feel that this momentum has been influenced by national developments. The apparent prescription in literacy and numeracy of not only what to teach but how and when, and even how long for, has led some teachers and schools to see teaching thinking as a way to retain their professionalism as they adopt (and adapt) new frameworks.

> Teaching thinking is an organic movement that has grown from the 'bottom-up' as teachers have tried the Approaches and Strategies in their classrooms.

Time

This is not to say that teaching thinking is an easy option. Particularly in the beginning, teachers have had to work hard to make links with the National Curriculum, school schemes of work and with the NLS and NNS Frameworks. In some cases they have had to convince sceptical head teachers that the ideas were sound and would be effective. Most ideas and activities need adapting to be successful, infusion takes even more time and effort to develop the resources more systematically and incorporate them in planning and schemes of work. This requires some commitment in terms of staff meetings and INSET time and funding. Neither of these is abundantly available in most schools. The schools we have worked with have, however, managed to find the time and money to support teaching thinking. If the will

> Enough schools and teachers have become involved to create a 'critical mass' for development as they have identified time and money from INSET plans and school budgets.

is there, the time and money follow (usually in that order too!). The role of the headteacher or head and senior management team is clearly crucial here. If development has the support and interest of school management for experimentation, to develop peer collaboration and find money for courses or training the teaching development is more likely to succeed and lead to a positive impact on pupils' learning.

Focus

We have not always been successful. Particularly in the early days it was difficult to advise teachers and schools on where to start and where to focus. Our commitment to teachers' involvment in such decisions made us tentative in our suggestions and this may have communicated a lack of conviction. Because our particular interest was in the process of implementation, we felt we would learn from a range of strategies and programmes. As our experience and understanding developed we recognised the limitations of published programmes for professional development. Our research indicated that what was successful about such materials was they way that they altered the language and discourse in classrooms, the way that the activities opened up pupils' thinking to teachers for mediation (or formative assessment) and the way the pupils perceived their own success at becoming 'better learners'. We learned that it was helpful to structure more precisely suggestions for getting started. We also learned to focus attention on pupils' responses more closely. Schools are awash with data about pupil performance these days; the difficulty lies in interpreting the data and knowing what to do differently tomorrow. Testing and targets are helpful; but it is action that is required to bring about improvement. Teaching thinking's close focus on teacher and pupil interaction or pupil and pupil talk is what provides for effective change.

Effective change

As with children's learning, the affective aspects of professional development are extremely important. Teachers' willingness to take risks and engage in a process of change is affected by their confidence, enthusiasm and motivation. All of these areas overlap and are interrelated. David Leat's conceptual model of competence is one way of understanding the interrelationships, particularly from a developmental perspective. This approach suggests that competence lies in the intersection of behaviours, knowledge and feelings. Teachers feel competent when they have adequate knowledge, adopt appropriate behaviours and are affectively comfortable. When they make a change in their practice they may have to change some of the automatic or routine behaviours to make the new approach work.

When development takes place a teacher starts to act outside this central area of perceived competence. This could be as a result of new knowledge, or attempting to try out new strategies and behaviours in the classroom. The change easily leads to feelings of discomfort. The resulting tension can mean that the aims of development are not achieved as a teacher struggles to act in the area of perceived 'competence'. If assimilating new knowledge or new teaching behaviours is too challenging then the easiest way to achieve a feeling of competence is to return to the previous comfortable state and reject the change. This is made worse if the change is externally imposed: the feeling of powerlessness caused by the lack of choice seems to make the negative feelings more acute. However, if the change is more actively chosen, the individual works harder to make the change work and assimilate the new ideas. The strategies in teaching thinking help to provide a structure for action and a focus for the teacher's attention (on pupils' response) that supports the changes in classroom behaviour.

> Teaching thinking
> Strategies help to scaffold
> or 'greenhouse' the process
> of change.

David Leat's conceptual model of competence

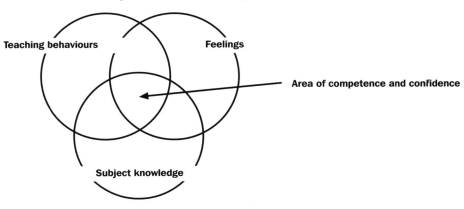

Maintenance

The first issue is how to cultivate behaviours which bear fruit without fertilising the 'weeds' that distract attention.

A growing challenge now is how to maintain a focus on teaching thinking. There are two key issues here. The first is how to sustain the enthusiasm that is generated by new ideas and activities as teachers become more familiar with the Strategies and Approaches. Many teachers are motivated by a new and practical idea for a classroom activity which can be acted upon. They want to act, to do something, preferably something that will help them with tomorrow's teaching! This can lead to trying out a plethora of strategies and moving from one to the next without identifying what it is about a technique that works and how it can be applied in the future. On the other hand, too much of a brake restraining the desire to try a new technique that might 'work', or too methodical an investigation dampens the enthusiasm needed to sustain the effort.

The ecology of development alters as you have a mix of mature plants or experts and the novice new seedlings.

The second issue is how to introduce or induct new colleagues to the approaches and ideas. We benefited from the genuine enquiry as we learned with the teachers and they learned form each other. This produced an intensity of interest which helped to drive the work forward. As some people become more familiar with teaching thinking they become more in the position of 'experts' communicating with 'novices'. This change in role alters the dynamics of communication.

Enaction research

The way we understand what is happening in teaching thinking is that it provides a space and a structure for many of the effective teaching behaviours outlined in *Chapter 11* to develop as the teacher focuses on understanding their pupils' thinking. The claims of a range of thinking skills approaches about pupil engagement, confidence and attainment are tested critically by classroom action. Teachers plan lessons to increase engagement in learning and need to listen carefully to how their pupils respond. The feedback they get from the pupils' enjoyment initially helps to sustain the changes in classroom behaviours. The further feedback provided by insights into pupils' understanding sets a series of teaching problems which can be tacked through mediation. This also feeds into short term planning over the next few lessons. They help the teacher to act, and in doing so, enact the findings of research on thinking skills, and more generally enact the findings from research into effective teaching.

Getting started

- Decide what you want to improve (eg use of the language for strategies in maths; questioning skills; aspects of comprehension such as inference; better use of connectives in writing etc, etc).
- Set a timescale (at least half a term, up to a school year).
- Choose ONE Strategy or Approach or ONE subject to infuse the Strategies into that should help (eg **Odd One Out; Community of Enquiry; Living Graphs; Writing Frames**).
- Collect some classroom data (eg using mental strategies sheet; pupils' questions; practice SATs inference questions).
- Use the Strategy or Approach once or twice a week. Make sure you include time for pupils to talk to each other as well as to the class. Include metacognitive review of the learning as pupils' familiarity with the Strategy or Approach improves.
- Collect data again half way through (to help focus the remaining lessons).
- Collect data again at the end.
- Analyse what happened. If there is improvement, what do you think caused it? The focused practice? Your extra time and effort? The pupils' discussion? Your understanding of their thinking? Would it have happened anyway?

Further reading

Higgins S. & Leat D. (1997) 'Horses for courses or courses for horses: what is effective teacher development?' in *British Journal of In-Service Education 23,3* pp 303-314 (ISSN 0305-7631)

Leat D. (1993) 'Competence, teaching, thinking and feeling' in Oxford *Review of Education 19,4* pp 499-510.

Leat D. (1999) 'Rolling the Stone Uphill: Teacher Development and the Implementation of Thinking Skills Programmes' in *Oxford Review of Education 25*

13

Metacognition
and learning

'*Reasoning involves both the ability to reason (in terms of what are often called thinking skills) and the disposition to reason with others (to be reasonable in one's argumentation)...A person lacking in either cannot be deemed rational*'

Matthew Lipman

13 Metacognition and learning

There is considerable debate about metacognition in the research literature. The coining of the term is usually attributed to Flavell (1976, 1977):

> 'Metacognition refers to one's knowledge concerning one's own cognitive processes and products or anything related to them... For example, I am engaging in metacognition (metamemory, metalearning, metaattention, metalanguage, or whatever) if I notice that I am having more trouble learning A than B; if it strikes me that I should double-check C before accepting it as a fact; ... if I sense that I had better make a note of D because I may forget it;... Metacognition refers, among other things, to the active monitoring and consequent regulation and orchestration of these processes ... usually in the service of some concrete goal or objective'
>
> Flavell, 1976, p 232

Some researchers enthuse about its importance and potential, others question the meaningfulness of the concept. Our reading and interpretation of this research base has influenced our thinking and work with teachers and pupils. The following summary of our readings and references should provide a practical starting point for those interested in applying the idea or learning more.

Build on what they know: learners need a knowledge base and can only use more sophisticated learning strategies when they relate new information to existing knowledge (Brown, Campione & Day, 1981; Weinstein & Mayer, 1986; Biggs, 1988; Carr, Alexander, & Folds-Bennett, 1994).

Model effective thinking: such as by thinking aloud or asking other pupils to talk through their thinking (Brown & Palinscar, 1987; Pressley, El-Dinary, Marks, Brown & Stein, 1992; Pressley, Harris & Marks, 1992; Mason, 1994).

Teach *for* strategies: learners need a variety of approaches and practice in applying appropriately. (Pressley, El-Dinary, Marks, Brown & Stein, 1992; Pressley, Harris & Marks, 1992).

Build *and then dismantle* the scaffold: teachers should support or 'scaffold' learners' first attempts at using new strategies, then remove the scaffolding as learners become more confident and proficient (Vygotsky, 1978; Brophy, 1992; Brown, 1984; Brown & Palinscar, 1987; Pressley, El-Dinary, Marks, Brown & Stein, 1992; Pressley, Harris & Marks, 1992; Cardelle-Elawar, 1995; Wray & Lewis, 1997).

Practise the use *and* application of Strategies: effective Strategies should be practised through a range of tasks and need 'reminders' over time (Brown & Palinscar, 1987; Pressley, El-Dinary, Marks, Brown & Stein, 1992; Pressley, Harris & Marks, 1992).

Process *and* outcomes: teaching needs to include the process of learning as well as the curriculum content (Berardi-Coletta, Buyer, & Dominowski, 1995).

Infusion works: strategies are best taught through the curriculum and in the context of classroom tasks (Brown & Palinscar, 1987; Borkowski, 1992; Pressley, El-Dinary, Marks, Brown & Stein, 1992; Pressley, Harris & Marks, 1992).

Teach *why* it works: learners should understand why the skills they are taught are helpful (Brophy & Good, 1986; Lampert, 1988; Pressley, Harris & Marks, 1992; Montague, Applegate, & Marquard, 1993).

Develop a disposition for learning: learners need to believe that, with sufficient effort and effective strategies, they can learn and understand challenging material (Pressley, El-Dinary, Marks, Brown & Stein, 1992; Jausovec, 1994).

References

Biggs J.B.
(1988) 'The Role of Meta-cognition in Enhancing Learning' in *Australian Journal of Education vol 32/2* pp 127-138

Berardi-Coletta B., Buyer L. S. & Dominowski R. L.
(1995) 'Metacognition and Problem-solving: A Process Oriented Approach' in Journal of Experimental Psychology – Learning, Memory, and Cognition, 21 pp 205-223

Borkowski J. G.
(1992) 'Metacognitive Theory: A Framework for Teaching Literacy, Writing, and Math Skills' in *Journal of Learning Disabilities, 25* pp 253-257

Brophy J.
(1992. 'Probing the Subtleties of Subject-matter Teaching' in *Educational Leadership 49*.7 pp 4-8

Brophy J. & Good T.L.
(1986) 'Teacher Behaviour and Student Achievemen' in Wittrock M.C. (ed.) *Handbook of Research on Teaching* New York: Macmillan

Brown A.L., Campione J. & Day J.
(1981) 'Learning to Learn: On Training Students to Learn from Texts' in *Educational Researcher*, 10.2 pp 14-21

Brown A.L. & Palincsar A.S.
(1987) 'Reciprocal teaching of comprehension strategies: A natural history of one program for enhancing learning' in Borkowski J.& Day J.D. (eds) *Cognition in special education: Comparative approaches to retardation, learning disabilities, and giftedness* Norwood, NJ: Ablex

Brown G.
(1984) 'Metacognition: new insights into old problems? ' in *British Journal of Education Studies 32*, pp 213-219

Carr M., Alexander J., & Folds-Bennett T.
(1994) 'Metacognition and mathematics strategy use' in *Applied Cognitive Psychology, 8* pp 583-595

Cardelle-Elawar M.
(1995) 'Effects of metacognitive instruction on low achievers in mathematics problems' in *Teaching and Teaching Education, 11* pp 81-95

Flavell J.
(1976) 'Metacognitive aspects of problem solving' in Resnick L. (ed) *The Nature of Intelligence* Hillsdale, NJ: Lawrence Erlbaum Associates

Flavell J. & Wellman H.
(1977) 'Metamemory' in. Kail R & Hagen J. (eds) *Perspectives on the Development of Memory and Cognition* Hillsdale, NJ: Lawrence Erlbaum Associates

Jausovec N.
(1994) 'Can giftedness be taught?' in *Roeper Review, 16* pp 210-214

Lampert M.
(1988) 'What Can Research on Teacher Education Tell Us About Improving Quality in Mathematics Education?' *in Teaching and Teacher Education 4,2* pp 157-170

Mason L.
(1994) 'Analogy, Metaconceptual Awareness and Conceptual Change: a classroom study' in *Educational Studies, 20,2* pp 267-291

Montague M., Applegate B., & Marquard K.
(1993) 'Cognitive strategy instruction and mathematical problem-solving performance of students with learning disabilities' in *Learning Disabilities Research and Practice, 8* pp 223-232

Palincsar A.S. & Brown A.L.
(1984) 'Reciprocal teaching of comprehension-fostering and comprehension-monitoring activities' in *Cognition and Instruction, 1* pp 117-175

Pressley M., Harris K.R. & Marks M.B.
(1992) 'But good strategy instructors are constructivists!' in *Educational Psychology Review,* *4* pp 3-31

Pressley M., El-Dinary P.B., Marks M.B., Brown R. & Stein S.
(1992) 'Good strategy instruction is motivating and interesting' in Renninger K.A., Hidi S., & Krapp A. (eds) *The role of interest in learning and development* Hillsdale, NJ: Erlbaum

Talizina N.F.
(1999) 'Psychological Mechanisms of Generalization' in Hedegaard M. & Lompscher J.(eds) *Learning Activity and Development* Aarhus: University Press

Vygotsky L.S.
(1978) *Mind in society: The development of higher psychological processes* Cambridge, MA: Harvard University Press

Weinstein C.E. & Mayer R.E.
(1986) 'The teaching of learning strategies' in Wittrock M.C. (ed.) *Handbook of Research on Teaching* (3rd ed) New York: Macmillan

Wray D. & Lewis M.
(1997) *Extending Literacy* London: Routledge

Zimmerman B.J.
(1989) 'Models of self-regulated learning and academic achievement' in Zimmerman B.J. & Schunk D.H. (eds) *Self-regulated learning and academic achievement: Theory, research, and practice* New York: Springer-Verlag

14
Creating resources with ICT

The whole of the developments and operations of analysis are now capable of being executed by machinery. ...As soon as an Analytical Engine exists, it will necessarily guide the future course of science.

Charles Babbage *Passages from the Life of a Philosopher (1864)*

14 Creating resources with ICT

Teaching with ICT: computers are tools. They can be used by the teacher for preparation of teaching resources or for presenting information and ideas.

Tools for teachers

Computers are tools for teachers to prepare resources and present their teaching. This might be with a desk-top publishing programme to prepare materials for mysteries or a writing frame. Microsoft's *Powerpoint* can be used to introduce ideas to a class or to share a text for the **Community of Enquiry**. Multimedia software can also be used to develop resources for teaching thinking. Programs to create Internet pages are getting easier to use all the time with the result that web-based resources can be easily created. These resources do not even have to be used over the Internet, though if you want to take advantage of the WWW for communicating this might be a reasonable long-term goal.

Tools for learners

Teaching through ICT: computers can also be used by pupils as part of the process of learning or to put together a product, or to communicate with others about their learning.

Once writing frames have been created on a computer, it is an easy step to turn them into a template or read-only file so that they can be completed on-screen. With a generic program like Microsoft *Word* it is also possible to make documents interactive using the forms tools with choices in drop-down lists. Other programs, such as concept mapping or mind mapping software are generic, though are clearly designed to support thinking and learning. *Inspiration* and *Mind Manager* are two examples of these programmess for older pupils and adults. Inspiration also produce *Kidspiration*, a visual mapping tool for 6 - 9 year olds which has the added bonus of speech to read out the text on screen.

Supporting subjects

Some software lends itself readily to thinking skills Strategies and Approaches. A program such as *Sim City* has a clear geographical focus for example, but can be used to develop understanding of important geographical concepts. Some of the software reissued by BECTA for the NNS for primary mathematics, such as *Monty*, *Playtrain* or *Toyshop* promote approaches to mathematics which can easily be developed through teaching thinking. One of the benefits of ICT is that such information is often available as pictures, video or sound and not just as text.

Thinking skills software

As the second ICT Exemplar in *Chapter 10* shows, there are programs specifically designed to teach thinking skills. The issue here is in finding such software and having the time to evaluate it to identify an appropriate niche in the school curriculum. The activities in these programs usually focus on sorting, matching and patterns for younger children then logical thinking and reasoning activities for older pupil. The *Thinkin' Things* series 1-3 (Edmark) offers a range of such activities. The main advantage is that the computer provides rapid, accurate feedback. With the top level of puzzles in the logical journey of the *Zoombinis* (The Learning Company) it can take you as long to work out what to do as the pupils! Other software is designed to support collaborative thinking and reasoning and a number of examples are available on the WWW such as *'Kate's Choice'* on the Thinking Together site and *'Atlantic Crossing'* on Northumberland LEAs Thinking for Learning site.

ICT as a catalyst for learning

ICT can be an effective part of the learning process. The provisional nature of work that can easily be changed is a real incentive for pupils to improve what they have done and for the teacher to focus pupils' attention on exactly what needs to be improved. For example the work put into creating a multimedia product can involve developing ICT skills, curriculum knowledge and thinking, as the first ICT Exemplar showed.

ICT for communicating ideas and information

Communication can also be enhanced using ICT: this is an exciting prospect at the present time. This can be for teachers, exchanging information and ideas using e-mail or websites, or for pupils to publish information on the Internet, ask questions of experts or exchange ideas with their peers. One example for this is *Newswise* where topical news stories are put up on the web as a basis for discussion and thinking. Pupils' ideas and opinions are exchanged on-line. Though this kind of approach is in its early stages and not without technical problems, the potential it offers is exciting.

Getting started...

ICT offers an efficient way to create, store and adapt teaching thinking materials and resources. Two support sheets are included in this appendix to help get you started. The sheets guide you through creating an **Odd One Out** task sheet (like *Resources 4 and 5*) and creating a **Writing Frame** (like *Resources 1, 2* and *3*) using Microsoft's *Word '97*. The menu options and toolbars will look slightly different if you are using *Office 2000* or *XP*.

Once you have created one resource it is easy to adapt the original file to create another task, but don't forget to use the 'Save As...' command or you will overwrite the original document.

Websites

Inspiration and Kidspiration **www.inspiration.com**

Newswise **www.dialogueworks.co.uk/**

Northumberland LEAs Thinking for Learning site **http://ngfl.northumberland.gov.uk/**

Thinking Together **www.thinkingtogether.org**

For further websites and information about teaching thinking available on the Internet see the *Appendix: Information on the Internet*.

Exemplar 1   # Odd One Out: using Clip-Art in *Word*

1. Create a new blank document. Open *Word* from the Start menu (if you can't see it at the bottom left corner of the screen, move the mouse down and it will appear as you hover over it).

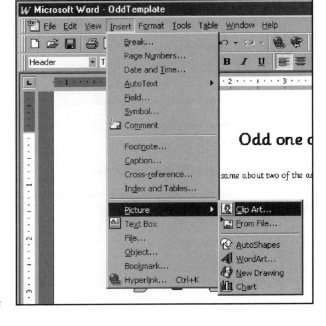

2. Type in the title of the worksheet. Adjust the font and size appropriately.

3. Choose Insert and Picture then Clip Art. Decide on the focus of the task.
Look through the range of pictures.
Add three or four pictures as appropriate for your activity.

   Tip: you may need to change the way the picture moves on the page. You can do this through the Format... and Picture... menus. Play around with the Wrapping and Position settings. These control whether the picture floats over the text or has text wrapped around it. You can also find these options by right clicking on a picture and choosing Format Picture... Uncheck the Float over text option on the Position tab. You can also get to these options by right clicking with the mouse on a picture.

4. Add any text you want the pupils to complete.

5. Save your work on your floppy disk. Print a copy.

Ideas for possible development:

- Add a header with space for pupils' names and the date (View menu - Header and Footer, add the text you want then Close the window.)

- Create a further activity by using the same pictures in a new document to make a set of sorting cards for a paired or group activity.

- Create a version of these sorting cards with their properties or attributes written on the back for pupils who need more support.

Designing writing frames using tables in *Word*

1. Sketch out a draft of your proposed writing frame on a piece of blank paper. Make sure you start with one large rectangle covering most of the page. This will make it easier to sub-divide with the table tools later.

2. Create a new document.

3. Open *Word* from the Start menu (if you can't see it at the bottom left corner of the screen, move the mouse down and it will appear as you hover over it).

4. If it is already open click on the *Word* icon at the bottom of the screen and choose <u>N</u>ew from the <u>F</u>ile menu.

5. If you want a landscape page, adjust the Page Set<u>u</u>p... from the File menu look for the Paper <u>S</u>ize tab and click on the appropriate radio button.

6. From the Table menu, choose Draw Table. The Tables and Borders toolbar should appear and your cursor will change to a pencil. This is the

   easiest way to draw complex tables. First, draw one large rectangle inside the margins of the page. To do this, drag diagonally from the top left to the bottom right to define the extent of the table - an outline of a rectangle appears as you drag the pen. (Note: if your table shrinks or disappears it is likely that your table goes outside the printable area of the page. If so, Undo your last few steps (Control and z is the shortcut) and re-draw the table making sure it is inside the grey ruler lines at the top and left side of the page.)

7. Next, draw in vertical and horizontal lines following your design. Add the text that you want in each of the cells in the table. Check that the font and size are appropriate.

8. You can use the rubber tool to remove lines from your table, or highlight cells and use the <u>M</u>erge Cells from the Table menu. You can also add more lines or use the S<u>p</u>lit Cells option.

9. Save your work on your floppy disk. Print out a copy.

Ideas for possible development:

- Add some clip art to make the writing frame more attractive (N.B. You can paste pictures into tables, but only when the pictures are treated as text - the box around the picture is a thin black line and it has black corners or 'handlers' when it is highlighted).

- Add some instructions in a text box which pupils can delete as they start to work. Click on the text box tool on the Drawing tool bar (if it is not visible, View, then Toolbars, then Drawing).

- Use the Forms toolbar (View, then Toolbars, then Forms) to add free text entry forms or pick lists.

Information on the Internet

Website addresses change regularly. If the any of the addresses below are no longer valid try a search for the name of the organisation or the resource. An up-to-date version of these links is available at: **http://www.staff.ncl.ac.uk/s.e.higgins/think/** or through **http://www.chriskingtonpublishing.co.uk/**

Interest in the UK in thinking skills has increased as a result of its inclusion in the National Curriculum. You can download a *Word* version of the DfEE report by Carol McGuinness **"From Thinking Skills to Thinking Classrooms"** **www.dfee.gov.uk/research/re_brief/RB115.doc** which was part of the thinking behind this revision. The DfEE Standards site has a section on thinking skills **http://www.standards.dfee.gov.uk/thinking** currently under development.

Sites and information about specific thinking skills programs

There are a growing number of sites about *Philosophy for Children (P4C)* and the Community of Enquiry such as Matthew Lipman's site the **Institute For The Advancement of Philosophy For Children** based at Montclair State University- Matthew Lipman's site **(http://chss.montclair.edu/iapc/homepage.html)** with links to the **Institute for Critical Thinking** **http://www.chss.montclair.edu/ict/homepage.html.**

The Society for the Advancement of Philosophical Enquiry and Reflection in Education **http://www.sapere.net/** is a UK based educational charity offering resources, conferences, and training in philosophy for children. A good starting point for further P4C links is Terry Godfrey's W3*P4C* site **http://www.p4c.net/.**

For an international flavour of the movement have a look at some of the links to work across the globe such as the Federation of Australian Philosophy for Children Associations **http://www.utas.edu.au/docs/humsoc/philosophy/postgrads/FAPCA.html** and the Argentinian branch of Philosophy for Children **http://www.izar.net/fpn-argentina/.**

Reuven Feuerstein's **International Centre for the Enhancement of Learning Potential** (ICELP) has its own website **http://icelp.org/Pages/What_is_IE.htm.**

There are links to examples of the 'instruments'. A good overview of his programme of **Instrumental Enrichment** can be found on North West Regional Educational Laboratory's web site which evaluates a range of school improvement programmes **http://www.nwrel.org/scpd/natspec/catalog/feuerstein.htm** used in the US.

Edward de Bono's catalogue of resources (such as *CoRT* and the *Thinking Hats*) is on-line **http://www.edwdebono.co.uk/debono/home.htm** and colour-coded like his six thinking hats.

Top Ten Thinking Tactics has brief information from the publisher **http://www.education-quest.com/catalogue/.** Click on the 'Thinking Skills' link about this programme, together with other thinking skills books and resources.

Alistair Smith's Accelerated Learning has its own web site **http://www.alite.co.uk/)** as does **Robert Fisher** **(http://www.teachingthinking.net/.**

Kings College, London have developed two thinking skills programmes **CASE** (Cognitive Acceleration Through Science Education) and **CAME** (Cognitive Acceleration Through Maths Education). These are aimed at secondary schools, though being developed for younger pupils. Information about **CASE** can be found at: **http://www.kcl.ac.uk/depsta/education/teaching/CASE.html.** And CAME similarly at: **http://www.kcl.ac.uk/depsta/education/teaching/CAME.html.**

Readings and research about teaching thinking

Teaching Thinking: an Introduction to the Research Literature is a paper by John Nisbet originally published in 1988 available on the web http://www.scre.ac.uk/spotlight/spotlight26.html. It is part of the Scottish Council for Research in Education (SCRE) Spotlights series, and worth checking out in its own right. Other relevant Spotlights are number 79 *'Can thinking skills be taught'* by Valerie Wilson http://www.scre.ac.uk/spotlight/spotlight79.html.

and number 82 *'Peer and Parent Assisted Learning in Reading, Writing, Spelling and Thinking Skills'* by Keith Topping http://www.scre.ac.uk/spotlight/spotlight82.html.

Teaching Thinking magazine http://www.teachthinking.com/, from Questions publishing, has a research section and accessible articles. You have to subscribe to get full access.

An **ERIC digest** http://www.ed.gov/databases/ERIC_Digests/ed385606.html. about teaching thinking is also available, though a little dated now.

Teaching Thinking Skills, http://www.nwrel.org/scpd/sirs/6/cu11.html. by Kathleen Cotton, is another entry in School Improvement Research Series at Northwestern University with information on a number of approaches.

Web resources for teachers and pupils

Northumberland LEA's **Thinking for Learning** http://ngfl.northumberland.gov.uk/ site has teaching thinking resources developed by teachers using many of the Strategies in this book.

Dialogue Works http://www.dialogueworks.co.uk/ produce **Newswise**, an on-line resource to promote thinking through news stories and **Storywise** a handbook by Karen Murris & Joanna Haynes for developing Community of Enquiry with young children. This is the updated version of *'Teaching Philosophy with Picture Books'* which inspired us to try out the Community of Enquiry with younger pupils in schools.

The **Thinking Together** site http://www.thinkingtogether.org.uk/ has resources linked to the book of the same name by Lyn Dawes, Neil Mercer and Rupert Wegerif. It is worth checking out for the resources and the decision scenario *'Kate's Choice'*.

Critical thinking skills: teaching materials produced by the MiningCo http://7-12educators.miningco.com/education/712educators/msub21.html. and aimed at secondary school teachers but with adaptable ideas.

There are many other sources of information if you search on the Internet. Try terms like 'critical thinking' (which is often used in the US) as well as 'thinking skills'. There is no guarantee you will find what you want, but a search can throw up useful results.

Further reading

In each of the chapters in the book has suggestions for finding further information or reading and we have provided more academic detailed references where we thought this was appropriate. These are not all repeated here, rather we have tried to pull together some key texts, academic books, professional articles and published programmes for teaching thinking and thinking skills. Most are mentioned above, though not all!

Published programmes and classroom resources

Blagg N., Ballinger M. & Gardner R.
(1988) *Somerset Thinking Skills Course Handbook* Oxford: Basil Blackwell

Dawes L., Mercer N & Wegerif R.
(2000) *Thinking Together: A Programme of activities for developing thinking skills at KS2* Birmingham: Questions Publishing

DeBono E.
(1992) *Teach Your Child to Think* London: Penguin

Feuerstein R., Rand Y., Hoffman M.B. & Miller R.
(1980) *Instrumental Enrichment: an intervention programme for cognitive modifiability* Baltimore: University Park Press

Fisher P.
(ed) (2001) *Thinking Through History* Cambridge: Chris Kington Publishing ISBN 1 899857 44 3

Fisher R.
(1996) *Stories for Thinking* Oxford: Nash Pollock ISBN: 1-89825-50-9

Fisher R.
(1998) *Teaching Thinking: Philosophical Enquiry in the Classroom* London: Cassell ISBN 030470065

Lake M. & Needham M.
(1993) *Top Ten Thinking Tactics* Birmingham: Questions Publishing Company

Murris K. & Haynes J.
(2001) *Storywise: Thinking Through Stories* Dialogue Works: Newport ISBN 1-903804-00-0

Leat D.
(1998) *Thinking Through Geography* Cambridge: Chris Kington Publishing ISBN 1 899857 42 7

Smith A., Call C. & Batton J.
(1999) The ALPS approach: *Accelerated Learning in Primary Schools* (revised edition) Stafford: Network Educational Press Ltd ISBN: 1-855390-56-6.

Swartz R. & Parks S.
(1994) *Infusing the teaching of critical and creative thinking into content instruction: A lesson design handbook for the elementary grades* California: Critical Thinking Press & Software

Books about teaching thinking and developing understanding

Adey P. & Shayer M.
(1994) *Really Raising Standards: Cognitive intervention and academic achievement* London: Routledge

Baron J.B. & Sternberg R.J.
(eds) (1987) *Teaching Thinking Skills, Theory and Practice* New York: Freeman

Bonnett M.
(1994) *Children's Thinking* London: Cassell

Coles M.J. & Robinson
(1989) *Teaching Thinking* Bristol: Bristol Press

Collins C. & Mangieri J.N.
Teaching Thinking: An Agenda for the Twenty-First Century
(1992) Hillsdale, NJ: Lawrence Erlbaum

Lipman M.
(1988) *Philosophy goes to School* Philadelphia: Temple University Press

Lipman M., Sharp A.M. & Oscanyan F.S.
(1980). *Philosophy in the classroom.* Philadelphia: Temple University Press

Newton D.
(2000) *Teaching for Understanding* London: Routledge/Falmer ISBN 0-415227-91-7

Quinn V.
Critical Thinking in Young Minds London: David Fulton

Resnick L.B. & Klopfer L.E.
(eds) (1989) *Toward the thinking curriculum: Current cognitive research* Alexandria, VA: Association for Supervision and Curriculum Development

Sharron H. & Coulter M.
(1994) *Changing Children's Minds* Birmingham: Imaginative Minds

Smith A.
(1998) *Accelerated Learning in Practice* Stafford: Network Educational Press

Splitter L.J. & Sharp A.M.
(1995) *Teaching for Better Thinking - The Classroom Community of Inquiry* Melbourne: ACER

White R. & Gunstone R.
(1992) *Probing Understanding* London: Falmer Press

Wood D.
(1998) *How Children Think and Learn* (2nd Edition) Oxford: Blackwell

Wray D. & Lewis M.
(1997) *Extending Literacy* London: Routledge

Academic articles about teaching thinking

Baumfield V. & Higgins S.
(1997) 'But no one has maths at a party': pupils' reasoning strategies in a thinking skills programme' in *Curriculum 18.3* pp 140-148

Baumfield V.M. & Oberski I.O.
(1998) 'What do Teachers Think about Thinking Skills?' in *Quality Assurance in Education, Spring Vol. 6:1* pp 44-51

Higgins S. & Baumfield V.
(1998) 'A Defence of Teaching General Thinking Skills' in *Journal of Philosophy of Education 32.3* pp 391-398

Jordan R.R. & Powell S.D.
(1991) 'Teaching Thinking: The Case for Principles' in *European Journal of Special Needs, 6.2*

Leat D.
(1999) 'Rolling the Stone uphill: Teacher Development and the Implementation of thinking skills programmes' *Oxford Review of Education 25*

Leat D. & Nichols A.
(2000) 'Brains on the Table: diagnostic and formative assessment through observation' in *Assessment in Education 7.1* pp 103-121

McGuinness C.
(1993) 'Teaching thinking: New signs for theories of cognition' in *Educational Psychology 13,3/4*

Other relevant articles

Black P. & Wiliam D.
(1998) 'Assessment and Classroom Learning' in *Assessment in Education 5.1*

Higgins S. & Leat D.
(1997) 'Horses for courses or courses for horses:' what is effective teacher development?' in *British Journal of In-Service Education 23.3* pp 303-314

Leat D.
(1993) 'Competence, teaching, thinking and feeling' in *Oxford Review of Education 19,4 pp 499-510*